Going for Gold

Change Your Life with NLP

– JIMMY PETRUZZI –

www.NLP-TrainingCourses.com
NLP Centre of Excellence
Free Phone: 0800 955 6808

An environmentally friendly book printed and bound in England by
www.printondemand-worldwide.com

Mixed Sources
Product group from well-managed
forests, and other controlled sources
www.fsc.org Cert no. TT-COC-002641
© 1996 Forest Stewardship Council

PEFC Certified

This product is
from sustainably
managed forests
and controlled
sources

www.pefc.org

This book is made entirely of chain-of-custody materials

www.fast-print.net/store.php

GOING FOR GOLD (SECOND EDITION)
Copyright © Jimmy Petruzzi 2014
www.nlp-trainingcourses.com

ISBN: 978-178456-012-6

A catalogue record for this book is available from the British Library

First published 2012 by
FASTPRINT PUBLISHING of Peterborough, England.
Second edition published 2014

We are all ordinary people, though ordinary people can sometimes do extraordinary things by shining a light in a dark room.

I would like to take this opportunity to thank all of my colleagues, clients, and students who have contributed to this book.

I would especially like to thank Sara Lou-Ann Jones, Andy Paschalidis, Dr. Tony Strudwick, Mark Hughes, Wyatt Woodsmall, Chris Casper, all the boys at Sky Sports Radio, Chris Butler, the guys at Real Coaching Radio Steve Toth and the team, Ang, Andy Hill, David Dias, Lee Murphy. The Mind Body Spirit team and everyone who ever supported my work.

To my daughter, my brother, sisters, cousin, aunty, uncle, my closest family and friends who are my inspiration.

Many elite athletes and sports people say, the mental aspects of sport make the difference between being a champion or not; as little as 1% can be the difference between being a world champion and being ranked 50th in the world.

In the game of life the margins of greatness and mediocrity are also minimal. The difference between succeeding and having a fruitful career, and an amazing life is minimal...

By transferring the same skills, principles and mindset that many of the world's best athletes and sports people use to be at the top of their game, we can help people in everyday life to help fulfil their potential.

In life all we have is the "here and now" and "making the most" of everything that comes our way. We can't relive our past, though we can take our past experiences and use them in a positive way. We can learn from failure and bask in our success.

The book is full of practical exercises on how to use your mind more effectively, using the mindset of champions, and techniques from NLP, hypnotherapy and other psychological strategies to gain more success in life and get the best out of yourself consistently. The book also has several real-life stories based on my experience of working with people linked to the techniques and strategies across a broad range of areas – business, sport, personal development – which helps you the reader understand the applications of the techniques and build an association to your life.

The book is intended to provide you with a resource to help fulfil your potential. The book provides the reader with techniques that focus on achieving results. If you're serious about achieving results this book is for you. Help get the best out of yourself and achieve more consistent results. Anything is possible. This book can help you discover your potential and obtain your dreams. You don't need to settle for anything less than what you want or what you want to be.

We are all special and have a lot to offer. Sometimes we need help to get started, with my coaching experience I know how to help people create a fulfilling life. If you don't wake in the morning happy and looking forward to your day, then you are missing out. What area could you improve? What is important to you? "The book" gets you out of an unhappy state and moves you to a new and higher level. The groundbreaking tools and techniques that you will learn will be with you for the rest of your life. There is no reason why you should ever be unsatisfied any longer.

The book works at the deepest level of our minds, and offers techniques that athletes use to get world-class results, helping people live extraordinary lives, reconnecting and finding their passions. A 65 year-old woman once came to me asking for help. She was living on her own and she had retired. Her life wasn't at all what she had been looking forward to. She had gained weight and isolated herself. Her life felt meaningless. She had medical issues such as arthritis and a poor-functioning thyroid. Her doctor had told her she'd probably not be able to lose much weight and that exercise, especially running, was out of the question.

Applying some of the techniques available in the book, in a way she'd never believed possible, she transformed her life, joining exercise groups and making new friends. She lost weight. She began running and most startling, she began enjoying swimming. She had spent her entire life avoiding water due to a deep-seated fear. She said that her life was truly transformed by activating her goal setting and using the tools and techniques during coaching. You don't have to be an Olympic athlete to achieve Olympic results.

The book takes you through techniques and strategies step by step. It is full of practical and interactive exercises and gives you examples of how these techniques have been used with people in business, sport, and to overcome life's challenges. So you can adapt the techniques to suit without too much theory and content, making the book very practical and user-friendly, which is unique.

Books written on improving mental and physical skills are generally theoretically based, which limits the application of using the book as a resource.

This is a "how to do" book, it is easy to follow, it has step-by-step instructions and examples people can relate to.

In fact to use an analogy, think of a satellite navigation system in a car. How many people are interested in the complexity of how the system works? How important and useful is it to know how it works? The most important thing to the consumer is knowing where they want to go and how to programme it. If we imagine our mind being similar to a satellite navigation system, then the tools in the book are a set of instructions there to assist you, the reader, to programme your mind to help you achieve the results you want in life. This is also a book which you can go back and use time and time again.

It's the Journey that makes the destination special

If climbing Mount Everest was easy, it wouldn't be such a beautiful experience. Life is about challenges. It's not always easy. We have to roll up our sleeves and get busy when faced with challenges. When we make it to the other side of our difficulties and we look in the mirror we see our truth, what we are capable of, and challenges get fewer and farther apart as we develop our confidence through realizing our capabilities. But sometimes we all need a little advice, support or an objective viewpoint.

This book is best used as a guide for you to help make the most out of life and create and make the most out of opportunities.

The Making of a Champion

Most people live ordinary lives

Just occasionally you meet someone who lives beyond the average - people who dare to not just dream but actually DO.

Despite difficulties and challenges that would cause most to give up, these individuals and their families have decided to think and live outside the box.

Then there are those who would dare to think of the well-being and safety of others and devote themselves to this service – sometimes risking their own lives to do so.

In a world of celebrities without character, there are diamonds if you are prepared to take notice. These are true champions. Watch, learn from and be inspired in your own life – because a champion is made not born.

Get busy living and make your life the best it can be. The most exciting it can be, and start your feet running with each new day. Be confident and positive and have all you want in your life. Persistence beats resistance. Do you have desire? Do you have passion? Get your mind going. Anyone can do anything.

Energy Flowing

Start out by getting your energy flowing. Punch the air. Give a big shout... Yoo-hoo! Now hold your arms out to the side and start circling them. Shout... Yes! Yes! Now circle one arm backwards and one arm forwards. Engage your brain by going different directions at the same time. Keep it going. Move your arms up and down, out to the side. Shout it out!

Accountability

Be accountable. Take your own life into your own hands. Look in the mirror and say: "I am responsible for where I am." When you acknowledge that, you are in power. You learn that you can make anything happen. In fact, no one else can. Rather than joining a club of people who don't accept responsibility, join with others who want to take charge.

Successful Failures

There are many "impossible" success stories. Michael Jordan, one of the world's most accomplished basketball players, didn't make his high school basketball team. Stephen King sent his first novel in for publication and was rejected over and over, until he finally gave up and threw it in the trash. His wife retrieved it and sent it in behind his back, "Carrie" was published and a prolific career began. The Beatles were denied a record deal. The Wright brothers were told they would never fly. Many who've lived in the most difficult surroundings have proven that odds can be overcome and success attained on a worldwide, historical level.

Overcoming Adversity

Helen Keller, born June 27, 1880. At age 19 months she went deaf and blind as a result of a short illness. At age six she could communicate with the young daughter of the family's cook through some of her own signs. By age seven, she had over 60 home signs to communicate with her family. Later, she was the first deaf-blind person to earn a Bachelor of Arts degree.

Helen's teacher, Annie Sullivan, who was visually impaired herself, broke through the isolation imposed by a nearly complete lack of language, allowing the girl to blossom as she learned to communicate. Helen became a prolific author. Others, such as Alexander Graham Bell and Charles Dickens, who both had invested energy working with deaf and blind children, were instrumental in helping Helen Keller on her journey as well.

Helen Keller inspired and changed the world for many others. She, and those who supported her, made huge advances that changed lives back then and still, to this day, she is an inspiration. She didn't do it alone, but had people who believed in her and cared about her and others who were models for her.

Helen Keller rose to the challenges she faced in life, a great example of finding your strength of character, keeping strong, holding your focus and then leaving the earth a better place for having been here. Helen left the earth on June 1, 1968, after having achieved more than most could dream. We all have the ability to go forward. We all can dream. Dreaming is creating.

The obstacles you face are the vehicle to your success, just like Helen Keller. She may have been deaf and blind, but it didn't stop her from achieving greatness. It might be argued that it spurred her forward and gave her a platform.

What is NLP?

DEFINITION OF NLP

Neurolinguistic Programming

Neuro

The nervous system (the mind), through which our experience is processed via five senses:

➜   Visual (Sight)
➜   Auditory (Sound)
➜   Kinaesthetic (Touch)
➜   Olfactory (Smell)
➜   Gustatory (Taste)

Linguistic

Language and other non-verbal communication systems through which our neural representations are coded, ordered and given meaning. Includes:

➜   Pictures
➜   Sounds
➜   Feelings
➜   Tastes
➜   Smells
➜   Words (Self-talk)

Programming

The ability to discover and utilize the programs that we run (our communication to ourselves and others) in our neurological systems to achieve specific and desired outcomes.

In other words, NLP is how to use the language of the mind to achieve specific and desired outcomes and improve our results.

NLP has three key benefits:

1.   Improving communication
2.   Changing behaviours (and beliefs)
3.   Modelling excellence

NLP is based on principles that are very different from traditional psychology. While traditional clinical psychology is primarily concerned with describing difficulties, categorising them, and searching for historical causes, NLP is interested in HOW our thoughts, actions, and feelings work together right now to produce our experience. Founded on the modern sciences of biology, linguistics, and information, NLP begins with new principles of how the mind/brain works.

Many people study NLP to help them become more effective in their chosen field or for their own personal development. Becoming more confident and motivated, the patterns can be employed across a wide area of applications ranging from fields as diverse as business, sport, education, team building, sales, marketing, personal development, leadership and coaching. NLP techniques provide the opportunity to grow and develop, helping us fulfil our potential and be the best we can be.

If it's not working change what you are doing

Our specific thoughts, actions and feelings consistently produce specific results. We may be happy or unhappy with these results, but if we repeat the same thoughts, actions and feelings, we'll get the same results. The process works perfectly. If we want to change our results, then we need to change the thoughts, actions and feelings that go into producing them. Once we understand specifically how we create and maintain our inner thoughts and feelings, it is a simple matter for us to change them to more useful ones, or if we find better ones, to teach them to others. As well as using a winning mindset throughout the book, we use techniques which are derived from NLP and human excellence.

Contents

The structure of the book is an easy to follow guide which you can use as a manual over and over again.

Chapters are as follows:

Chapter 1: Taking Responsibility

Many of us focus on our negative pasts, what we've done wrong, wrongs that have been done to us. Think about listening to a song you don't like, or a movie that doesn't interest you. You wouldn't keep listening to them over and over. So, why do we do that exact thing with our past? With past issues, we need to acknowledge them, learn our lesson from them and then focus our attention on a new outcome that is going to make us feel the way we want and how we can express our unique gift to the world.

Chapter 2: Understanding our Behaviour

Some of that success can be understood by knowing how the mind works. There are two parts to the mind – the conscious and the subconscious. The conscious part is aware and allows us to experience the conditions that surround us. We see the people nearby. We see the environment, for good or not as good. The subconscious part is the part that lies under the surface. If you think about an iceberg, the subconscious part is what you can't see, the part that lies below the surface. It still has a weighty effect, but you don't really know by looking. You know it's there because of the way it influences the situation. Imagine how differently the chunk of ice would move about the ocean if it had nothing under the surface.

Chapter 3: Breaking Bad Habits

To create a new balance when stuck in an old pattern, we need to find our own life's path. Amid the pressure and anxiety we all face, it can be difficult. Start making changes by asking yourself what you want and what you have to offer. Then begin to focus on the positive and not the negative.

Chapter 4: Realigning Yourself

The key to satisfying human needs is to align with the individual's goals. Aim at accomplishing those goals. Each of us has an identity, or core values. Wake up to who you are. "Roll up your sleeves. Get off your backside, go out there and achieve your dreams! Your life truly can make that transformation in an instant. If you keep doing what you're doing for the next 25 years, will you be able to say you're happy at the end?"

Chapter 5: Dare to Dream

What transformation would you make? What would you like to do? Play the guitar or drums, build a satisfying relationship, run a marathon, write a book, or become a model? The things that inspire and create happiness cannot be bought. Wake up and live the life of your dreams. Begin your transformation.

Chapter 6: Setting Goals and Staying Motivated

Fast forward to the end of your life. "You have one week left. What would you do?" Grab a pencil and write down all the things you wished you had achieved and attempted in your life. "Who would you spend time with? What would you change? What were you here for? What was your sense of purpose? Who would you like to meet, to visit with? What impact would that person have on your life? What would you like to learn?"

Chapter 7: Self-Talk

We are often our own biggest critic, some of the things we say to ourselves we wouldn't say to anyone else.

Self-talk is important. Staying positive in the messages you hear and tell yourself has an impact on what happens and what you do. As a coach, I wouldn't tell my players, "Don't lose the ball." I would say, "Keep possession." If I say, "Don't lose the ball," the first thing the team will do is lose the ball. I will teach you how to focus on your strengths, not your weaknesses. The mind is powerful. Learn to be in control. Reach the peak of Mount Everest. Make your own powerful transformation. Build the life you deserve.

Chapter 8: Metaphorically Speaking

Using the power of metaphors to overcome challenges and obstacles.

Chapter 9: Believe in Yourself

J.K. Rowling, author of the Harry Potter books, lived in a United Kingdom council estate before the books were published.

There are many "impossible" success stories. Michael Jordon, one of the world's most accomplished basketball players, didn't make his high school basketball team. Stephen King sent his first novel in for publication and was rejected over and over, until he finally gave up and threw it in the trash. His wife retrieved it and sent it in behind his back, "Carrie" was published and a prolific career began. The Beatles were denied a record deal. The Wright brothers were told they would never fly. There are many stories of people who break through limitations. Believing in ourselves even when others don't is important to success.

Chapter 10: Getting into Shape

Being in shape is our greatest asset, our health and vitality is essential. Tools and techniques to get into shape in an enjoyable way can be found here.

Chapter 11: See Things from a Different Point of View

How to see things from a different point of view, to learn and grow.

Chapter 12: Modelling Excellence

Learn the difference that makes a difference, learn from the best in their field and elicit strategies for yourself.

Chapter 13: State of Mind, Getting in the Zone

How to be in the right state of mind at the right time.

Chapter 14: Time Out

Taking time to recharge the batteries.

Chapter 15: The Power of Visualisation and Imagery

Seeing is believing. The power of imagination.

Chapter 16: Proximity

Your net work is your net worth; make yourself associate with the right people.

Chapter 17: Laughter

The power of a good sense of humour.

Chapter 18: Letting Go of the Past

Moving into the future. Letting go and breaking free of the past and moving into a positive future.

Table of Contents

Introduction

This book was intended to provide people with a resource to fulfil their potential. This book provides the reader with techniques that focus on achieving results. If you're serious about achieving results this book is for you, to help get the best out of yourself and achieve more consistent results.

Anything is possible. This book can help you discover your potential and obtain your dreams. You don't need to settle for anything less than what you want or what you want to be.

Before you begin on this journey of finding your purpose and fulfilling your potential let's do a simple exercise.

Fast forward to the end of your life. "You have one week left. What would you do?"

Grab a pencil and write down all the things you had wished you had achieved and attempted in your life.

"Who would you spend time with? What would you change? What were you here for? What was your sense of purpose? Who would you have liked to meet, or visit? What impact would that person have on your life? What would you like to learn?"

My Story

I remember coming home from school one day in my last year of school disillusioned. I wasn't doing great academically at school.

I really wanted to be a sports star though at best I was mediocre in my ability at sport. I was a late developer, physically quite short in stature and very lean. Growing up was quite a lonely experience. My parents had emigrated from Italy to Australia to find work. And being the youngest child and not having other family around us, at times I felt isolated. My parents worked hard in non-skilled jobs for little pay. So money was tight.

It was a few months before leaving school and I had no real idea of what I was going to do.

I noticed my brother reading a book written by motivational speaker, Tony Robbins, and that's pretty much what my introduction to personal development and NLP was.

I then became interested in all things "personal development", did many courses, attended loads of workshops and read just about every book going.

I tried my hand at a few courses at college and dropped out; until I finally found something I enjoyed, communication, psychology, NLP.

I started to believe in myself and decided I was going to give a sports career my best shot, and my aim was also to help inspire disadvantaged children.

I tried my hand at many jobs, I remember doing a sales job were I worked endlessly for two weeks and didn't get paid. Finally I got a bit of a break and got a position working as a mail deliverer for the public service. It wasn't the best job though it gave me time to train as hard as I could physically. My dream was to play professional football in Europe. I put my head down trained hard and saved enough money to travel to Europe and try my hand at playing pro football.

Along the way I found myself excelling at running with the help of a good coach.

I had travelled to Italy and trialled with a few teams, until my sports career took me to Romania, the UK and the USA. I ended up back in the UK and things were going well. I was working as an athlete with a great conditioning coach. I was studying all things NLP, every course I could find, and many other sports courses, things were going well. I had a part-time job as a personal trainer and was playing a good standard of football and running some amazing sprint times. I had completely turned my life around and was helping other people turn their life around as a coach.

I had moved to London and had a fantastic position working with several footballers from some of the biggest clubs and the who's who. We trained celebrities, big CEOs, famous people; it was an amazing experience, a big learning curve. I carried on studying and commenced a distance learning course at Loughborough University; life was amazing I was living in London which was buzzing.

I was living the dream; my goal was to participate at the Olympic Games which were going to be held in Sydney where I grew up.

I had flown back to Sydney to visit my family for the first time in a few years, and make inroads into participating at the Olympic Games which were to be held a year later.

The trip was going well, it had been nice to see my family and friends and they were pleased for me. Then one evening I had participated in a football match, after the game I developed a huge headache and aching back which was indescribable. The next morning I had woken up and my head and back ache were getting worse and I collapsed. My sister had taken me to hospital, and they had conducted several tests and scans which were being assessed. No one could get to the bottom of what was wrong. However the head and back aches had eased off and I felt better.

I took it easy for the rest of the trip, rested and headed back to the UK, arriving in Manchester.

I headed back to London and it was not long before the head and back aches appeared again; to the point I was really struggling. I had seen several specialists and still things were inconclusive. I left my position in London and headed to Manchester with my partner at the time and near to family I had in the UK.

Things got progressively worse and I was at the point where I could barely get up a flight of stairs.

My dreams were shattered, I didn't know what to do, and I could barely stand up. My dreams of the Olympics about a year away were still in my mind.

Though time was running out, I went from being a top-class sports person, to struggling to walk up a flight of stairs. As time went by, I had seen every specialist and goodness knows what else and still no answers. As time progressed I just wanted the world to swallow me up, there were times I would go to sleep and wish not to wake up, my dreams were shattered.

I didn't know what to do, I was afraid, sad, stunned, I realised how fragile life was, one day you can have it all and one day it can all get taken away.

Everything I had worked for was lost, I didn't have any answers. I was devastated, all those years training, and the hard work I put in amounted to nothing. Things were not improving.

Then my life changed forever, my partner I was seeing at the time told me she was pregnant. What should have been great news, the best news I ever heard, also raised more fears. Time was going by, I was still getting these excruciating headaches and back pain, which made it hard to stand up sometimes.

It wasn't just about me, what was I going to do about becoming a parent in the state I was in?

Time passed, my daughter was born and it was the most amazing experience ever. The uncertainty about my future was still there, though whatever my prognosis I was going to make the most of spending time with my daughter. The Olympics came and I would get up in the early hours of the morning and watch it on TV with my daughter.

The pressure had eventually taken its toll, I had split with my partner, I had no job, I was heavily in debt, and had completely lost everything.

Though I achieved a milestone; I managed to walk to the post office which was 100 yards away, and that gave me some hope.

And gradually the walk to the post office became a walk to the local shop; I had changed my philosophy on life.

I was going to go for it, I changed my diet; I went from years earlier as an athlete being careful with what I ate, to eating whatever I liked within reason. Much more relaxed about things I decided it was now or never. I began feeling better, bit by bit, though the impact of those three years in my life would shape my life forever. I realised if there's anything you want to do, do it while you can, because you never know in life. So I made a pledge to live every day to the fullest and seize every moment.

I gradually got better, to the point I could start getting my life back. I took a job as a part-time teacher, and completed my teacher training course.

I got back into working in football with Bury Football Club's youth team. It wasn't the biggest club though it was a start, and carried on studying, and teaching.

I was getting my life back; at that point I made a decision I was going to teach NLP courses though I was going to do things differently. I was going to take the courses to a new level and make them accessible to everyone, after all people who can't afford the extortionate fees some training companies were and are charging would benefit from learning NLP too.

And one thing I realised when I wasn't well is I saw right through many of the people I had come across in the field of NLP and personal development; so many people on an ego trip and just in it for money.

I would do things differently, I would make changes. To me it became apparent after all the studies I did, all NLP was was just a set of skills taken from other aspects of psychology, hypnotherapy and other forms of therapy, learning and successful people, and given a label.

I would take things further, though first I had unfinished business. I wanted to succeed to the highest level in my career. Before I began teaching courses, I wanted to be the best I could be and be one of the best, if not the best in the world, not just at teaching – at applying.

I was back in full swing though I had learned a lot and I was determined to make a difference.

So I sat down and wrote my goals and what I wanted my life's purpose to be.

I went away for a week, and wrote and wrote and wrote.

I was passionate about sport, and helping people, and I felt I was in the right place to do so.

I wanted to reach as many people as I could and I wanted to help as many people as I could, and I felt I could achieve that by means of radio, seminars, conferences, courses and one-to-one work.

My work at Bury was going well, we were producing many talented young players, we drew a lot of attention to what we were doing; how could a club so small be developing so many players? Then, the first team was bottom of the league, by ten points and new management came in. With new management my opportunity came to literally perform a miracle and help the team get off the bottom of the league and stay up. We did it and many other opportunities would come my way; I got involved in working with international teams, and became a specialist at helping teams turn their plight around. I had helped Blackburn Rovers, Accrington

Stanley and worked with many other individuals in many other sports.

I was also working with people helping them to overcome fears, phobias, overcoming limiting and negative beliefs. I carried on studying, reading, and interviewing as many people as possible to find out what made some people successful in certain areas where others would struggle; learning how was it possible to help other people achieve excellence.

I was doing what I really enjoyed. I remember sitting down one nice September day when I had a minor extra role in the remake of the film Alfie, which starred Jude Law, Susan Sarandon and Marissa Tomei, thinking I've managed to turn things around, though this time things would be different, I would make a real difference.

Then an opportunity came to work with young offenders and deliver elements of CBT (Cognitive behaviour therapy) and interventions to staff working with young offenders and I took it.

This was possibly the most demanding, yet most rewarding position I had had, as I was working with young people who had experienced some of the most difficult circumstances, and every difference I could make was rewarding.

It was at that point I decided to deliver courses to the wider public and I was writing for an association for NLP which was founded by someone in America. I did so for free, and the founder of this association had been invited to deliver a course in the UK which I helped deliver components of for free, as I was passionate about NLP and helping people. Although the founder of this association pocketed a fortune I thought credit to him, it was a good course, we did a good job.

We were in discussions about a new course and all that was mentioned was money, and the courses seemed to be never ending, once you did one, you could do another, with what seemed to be recycled stuff to me.

It was from that moment I realised and saw through the way things were being run, NLP was an unregulated field, there were some excellent people doing some excellent work, though many people saw it as a money spin-off.

One association was always claiming to be better than another, there were associations springing up everywhere, and as long as you had the money, you could do a course, regardless of who you were – you could be an axe murderer for all anyone cared.

I even heard stories of people attending half a course with a well-known trainer and still receiving a certificate.

Courses being run with hundreds of people in the audience, being charged a fortune.

I was a teacher I had been used to high standards, that was when I decided we would work extensively to deliver a new cohort of courses through ILM, a division of City and Guilds who had been going over 100 years. Getting our courses approved and endorsed through them meant proper standards, class sizes, accommodating learning styles, and meeting a high level of curriculum standards.

It took a lot of hard work though once we achieved it, it was fantastic.

My next step was to formalise NLP in a way that would create our quality standard. Here were some powerful techniques and strategies that were learnt from some of the most successful people in their field that were falling into the hands of practically anyone who could afford to pay to do the courses. Which were in my view ridiculously priced, people paying even up to seven to ten thousand pounds for a course which wasn't even a qualification, as NLP wasn't regulated.

I was determined to change that, as my goal was and is, for NLP to be recognised as an effective intervention strategy by government regulation.

With that recognition NLP could be used on a broader scale to help many more people.

So I interviewed some of the best minds I could find in education, NLP, psychology and hypnotherapy. My search was extensive; I interviewed and discussed with several people the need for an association to be in place with the strictest measures.

And after four years development, I had developed with the help of many people along the way, the International Association of NLP and Coaching, which would lead the way with the tightest measures in place the use of NLP interventions and the teaching of it, and would also give people the opportunity to learn at an affordable level, and apply and teach the skills in the area of their expertise. The association would ensure ongoing development and best practice meetings, carry on with the development of the field, and whilst opening learning, would ensure people who used the skills worked to a strong code of ethics.

Whilst developing in the field of NLP, I co-developed the seminar, 'Get busy living' with Sara Lou-Ann Jones, who was this bundle of energy. We delivered the seminar around the world with the intention of spreading some positivity with the backdrop of a world being gripped by a recession.

I was on a seminar tour in Australia, driving in to a radio station to do a show early in the morning, it was my birthday, and after the radio show I was going in to do a talk at the high school I attended many years earlier, then I had a meal planned with family and friends in the evening.

It dawned on me, although I didn't have time to digest everything; I was living a life with a strong sense of purpose; I had achieved and was achieving many of the goals I set, when things seemed like there was no hope, though at the time I had the faith to believe I could turn things around.

And on my flight back to the UK, I looked out the window as we made our journey over several countries, thinking of all the places I had been and all the places I was going to go.

My purpose for the book is to share some powerful techniques, tools, strategies and a few stories that I have been fortunate enough to share with many people around the world to help them become the best they can be.

We are all born and blessed with powerful resources and the ability to achieve the most amazing things when we use our mind effectively.

The powerful techniques, tools and strategies in this book have given the opportunity for many people to get the best out of themselves, discovering and realising their true potential. This book will help you find the strength and character to rise to challenges, overcome limiting beliefs and break through obstacles.

Life is not a rehearsal, this is it, find your purpose and live your dream.

Your journey begins in the next chapter with taking full responsibility for your life.

Chapter 1: Taking Responsibility

Victim Thinking

Two long-time golfers were standing overlooking the river getting ready to hit their shots. One golfer looked to the other and said, "Look at those idiots fishing in the rain."

In our society there has always been a tendency to attribute our feelings to the behaviour of others.

My partner enquired as to why I don't play snooker with John any more. I asked her, "Would you continue to play with a guy who always gets drunk, takes ten minutes to take a shot, who tells lousy jokes while you are trying to pot and generally offends everyone around him in the snooker hall?" "Certainly not, dear," she replied. "Well, neither would he."

Some people believe that their emotions are inevitably caused by the actions of others; many people have become a generation raised to fear and blame.

The belief that "they" cause our feelings begins at a young age, is confirmed throughout our teenage years, and becomes our unquestioned reality. So the weather it gets me down, she irritates me, he upsets me, my job stresses me, the government doesn't look after me, and you're ruining our relationship!

Our aim is to become aware of how we respond to outside circumstances and to exercise more choice in our responses.

So if somebody typically "makes" us feel good we choose to accept and thoroughly enjoy this. And if somebody typically "makes" us feel upset or irritable we choose to cease co-operating in this. In essence, our aim is to develop our ability to "drive our own bus" instead of being passive passengers.

Do you make excuses or are you always looking for people to blame for your circumstances? Or do you do the running, do you take control of the situation, do you become empowered and stronger than you were before?

In NLP we talk about people living either at "Cause" or "Effect". If you are at effect you may blame others, or circumstances for your bad moods, or for what you have not achieved, or for your life in general. You may feel powerless or depend on others in order for you to feel good about yourself or about life. – If only my spouse, my boss, my co-workers, my parents, my children... understood me and helped me achieve my dreams, or did what I wanted or what is best for me, then life would be great. If you wait and hope for things to be different or for others to provide it, then you are at effect or a victim of circumstances. And really, how much fun is that? And how much fun do you think it is for others to be around you? Believing that someone else is responsible, or making them responsible for your happiness or your different moods is very limiting and gives this person some mystical power over you, which can cause you a great deal of anguish.

Being at cause means you have choices in your life – you can choose what is best for you while ensuring the choice is beneficial for those around you, those in your community and your society. That is, you consider the consequences of your actions on others, while not taking responsibility for their emotional well-being – believing you are responsible for the emotional well-being of someone else places a heavy burden on you and can cause a great deal of stress.

Those who live their lives at effect often see themselves, or live their lives, as victims with no choices whatsoever. The irony is that they do have choice and they have chosen not to choose but to be responsive to whatever is given to them.

Exercises

List three areas of your life you are living at cause. (Where you do the running.)

List three areas of your life you are living at effect.

(And would like to change, e.g. my job is making me unhappy, I can never find the right partner.)

By changing your attitude and accepting responsibility you feel more empowered and in control.

One of the exercises I do with my clients is the responsibility contract, to put them in the driver's seat.

Taking responsibility for your life.

Responsibility Contract

I hereby take full responsibility for my life from today onwards.

You can either live your life out of cause or effect. True winners take responsibility and under some of the most difficult circumstances turn things around to their advantage.

Life is about looking at the big picture, it is easy to lose track of the big picture.
Sign the contract.

Whatever the situation in your life, at whatever point you are, you can turn things around. Of course life isn't always fair, how do you explain some of the injustices of this world?

There are a lot of things in life I cannot explain and I don't have any reasoning for. I wouldn't be human if I said some situations and stories my clients share with me, some of the things I see in the news, I read in the papers didn't upset me. Of course I think we all go through times where we question certain things, question perpetrators of horrific crime, question God's work, question the government, our friends, family and even ourselves.

I don't profess to know all the answers, or any answers for that matter. However life is short and all in all does anyone really know the meaning of it all?

What does anyone know about anything other than what we're told or read?

The only thing for certain is that we are only on this planet in our present form for a short time. And we owe it to ourselves to make the most of every situation, every millisecond.

Life can be very challenging at times and we have all got a story to tell, some people tend to tell it more than others, dwell in the past, spend a lifetime going over the same problems and stories, though never do anything to change it.

Sometimes you don't get dealt the best cards in life, though we have a choice in how we respond. And it is within our response that our lives are shaped.

Chapter 2: Understanding our Behaviour

"Behaviour is a mirror in which everyone displays his own image"

Johann Wolfgang von Goethe

Our behaviours: Why do we do what we do?

We are a product of our thoughts.

What makes you unique, what influences your behaviour, why do you do what you do, what makes you the person you are?

Are some of your behaviours serving you and some having a negative impact on your life?

In my experience of working with many clients across a broad range of areas, I embarked on a journey to understand behaviour. I have always felt if I could understand what influences people's behaviour then I could get through to the true essences of a person. Underneath the layers so to speak, the layers people put on to disguise who they really are from the bottom of their heart and the depth of their soul. In my journey I attended many courses, read many books, studied thousands of people over many years, and over time I began to understand the concept that people aren't their behaviour.

Behavioural traits are influenced by many factors we will discuss later. The nature versus nurture debate will always rumble on and who is to say who is right or wrong? The one thing for sure is there are key moments in our life that shape the person we become. From the early stages in our life from the moment were born to the interaction with our parents and the closest people around us through to the imprints the closest people leave on us with their interactions with us. Then as a few years go by we begin to model certain actions of the people around us; parents, family, teachers, and our role models.

How many people are inspired to go on and become a sports star, a musician, dancer, or a certain career path, by being inspired by someone at an early age? Or as you become a parent yourself do you find yourself saying the same thing to your children that your parents said to you?

Then as we get into our teens and beyond our social groups begin to influence us, the people we socialise with have an impact on our lives. Their beliefs about the world, their aspirations, their social status, all rub off on us and influence our behaviour.

My journey into understanding human behaviour became a paradox. It was very simple, yet very complex, the result of a person's thoughts and feelings based on their interpretation of an event or set of circumstances, would produce a result. And this ongoing process would continue throughout people's lives. My journey helped me to understand the complexity and base for people's behaviour.

By understanding the process of why people did what they did, why people behaved in certain ways – if it wasn't a productive behaviour – the understanding enabled me to help them and we could change it to something more productive.

In my experience of working with people looking to, lose weight, give up smoking, become happier, overcome addictions and substance misuse, be free from anxiety or free from depression, overcome self-harming, and many other behavioural traits which are causing them harm, understanding the person's behaviour helped move them to more productive behaviour. The important factor is to separate the behaviour from the person. People aren't always behaving in one way all the time. People aren't always overeating; they don't smoke every minute of every day. People don't always react in the same way to certain events and situations. There are other factors involved in the thought process whose end result is a behaviour, which we will discuss shortly in this chapter. Its relevance can be very powerful in helping us understand ourselves better. Even within families and siblings behaviour can be vastly different. I am sure we have all come across, or at least read about, families who adopt a set of behavioural patterns which see their lives shaped in a completely different way. Families of which one sibling becomes a successful business person, another turns to drugs.

Our reactions to certain events constantly produce unusual behaviour. I remember working with an aspiring sports star who had completely lost their way, after a member of their family had been shot in gang-related crime. After the same incident another member of his family decided to pursue a career in law, he felt this was a way to bring justice to other people in similar situations. And another member of this sibling group had given up a lucrative business career to become a member of a gang to gain revenge. All three had behaved differently to this tragic event. I guess all three had their own reasons for their actions. Just as I guess all people, everyone has their own reasons for their behaviour, whether it's serving them or not.

Let's take a moment to think

Why do we do what we do? It is safe to say most people who smoke are well aware of the dangers of smoking, however they carry on smoking.

Most people know what foods to eat, that exercise is good for them. Let's explore and gain an understanding of why we do what we do, and by gaining that understanding we can change any negative patterns which aren't helping you live your life to the fullest.

Perception

Complete the following exercise.

What does the word relationship mean to you?

Now ask five different people what the word relationship means to them, and take note of the answers.

Is everybody's answer different?

Have you ever watched a programme on TV, then gone into work the next day and had a completely different perception of the programme to that of your work colleagues?

If you had two different sets of fans watching a football match and the referee gave a close decision for a penalty to one team, would both sets of fans' reactions be the same?

Why do people respond differently to different situations?

Have you ever heard the expression, "that person lives in their own world"?

Well we all live in our own world which is unique to us. What forms that unique experience and influences our behaviours, thoughts and feelings? The key factors are our filters, how we process information and interpret the information. (We will discuss each category later in the chapter first we will look at how these components influence our behaviour.)

- ➔ Our language
- ➔ Memories
- ➔ Attitudes
- ➔ Values and beliefs
- ➔ Decisions
- ➔ Meta programs
- ➔ Time/space, matter
- ➔ Energy

How do the above components influence our behaviour?

The explanation is as follows

We have established we all make sense of the world in our own way. Our interpretations to events that are going on outside us are perceived differently from person to person; as a result the behaviours that people manifest are also different.

First think about what is going through your mind at this present moment in time, this very second. Think about all the thoughts and feelings that are going through your mind this second. What are we aware of, the objects around us, our past, our future, our life, and the many thoughts which pass through our mind?

The things we stop and think about passing through our mind; what is for tea, have I put the bins out, I should make that phone call later, what's on TV tonight, I might go for a drive, the list goes on. What are some of the things we notice and don't notice; different thoughts come into our mind at different times depending on what we focus on. And at a conscious level we are limited to how many things we can focus on, let me explain.

Our Conscious Awareness

It is estimated that your brain receives about four billion nerve impulses every second. Are you consciously aware of all of this information? No! For example, are you aware of how your feet feel on the floor? Unless you have sore feet I suspect that you were not aware of how your feet felt until I mentioned it. Why? Because it was not important at the time and it was filtered out. Of the four billion bits of information, you are only consciously aware of about 2,000 bits, or about 0.00005 per cent of all the potential information. To take in and process more of this information would either drive you crazy or be such a distraction that you could not function.

Do you consciously remember every step you perform driving in to work in the morning, the traffic lights you stop at, the gear changes, the people, shops you drive past?

So of all the billions of nerve impulses our mind receives every second, how do we interpret the information the way we do? How and why do we all see things differently and what is the impact it can have on our life? How do we decide to interpret the information?

What are the key components in breaking down this information to a manageable level in order for us to make sense out of it? Of the four billion nerve impulses that hit our mind every second, all of our past memories, and future plans, every event that is happening, all our interests, we filter, delete, distort, and generalise this information to the point we can make sense of it.

Filters – Deletions, Distortions and Generalisations

What happens to all of this other information? It is filtered from your conscious awareness by deleting (e.g. how your feet feel against the floor), distorting (i.e. simplifying) or generalising. What you actually delete, distort and generalise depends on your Beliefs, Language, Decisions, Values, Memories, and Meta Programs.

For example your perception of a certain event can be completely different based on the part of the world you live in, your gender, your religion, your experiences. Let us look at a few examples to gain an understanding of how they work.

Beliefs

Suppose you have a belief that "you are unattractive or you're not a clever person". How would you react when someone approaches you and says, "You look very nice in that shirt or dress," "That was an intelligent point,"? Depending on the circumstances, you may dismiss, discount or deflect their positive feedback. Internally, you may think they have not looked at it in detail and when they do, they will find something wrong and change their opinion.

Suppose all day, people tell you that you you're attractive or you're clever – do you really hear them? Not likely! And then one person points out that your nose looked a bit big on those holiday pictures, or the point you made at work last week was a bit odd. Does this resonate for you? You bet it does! It verifies your belief about yourself. From a "filter" perspective, you have deleted and distorted the positive feedback and focused on the negative. What beliefs do you have about yourself, about others, about the world, that limit who you can be or what you can accomplish?

Language (Words)

Words are a form of code to represent your interpretation of something. Try this exercise, get a group of people together and have each independently write down five words that for them means "exercise". I will bet that nobody comes up with the same five words as you do; and as a group you may not have any words in common. The word "exercise" is code for what exercise means for you and I suspect that your friends have a completely different meaning for this word.

A perfect example is relationships. We enter into long and sometimes heated discussions with our loved ones about "our relationship", without ever really discussing what "relationship" means to each other.

Decisions

You make decisions (i.e. generalise) so that you do not have to relearn things every day. If you want to make a cup of tea, you learned a long time ago (made the generalisation) that you turn on the kettle, place a tea bag in the cup – you do not have to go through the whole process of relearning how to make a cup each and every time. Generalisations are useful and they can also get us into trouble.

How many of us know how to open a door? In an experiment, researchers put the doorknob on the same side of the door as the hinge. What do you think happened when they left adults in the room? They would go up to the door, grasp the doorknob, twist and then try to push or pull the door open. Of course, it would not open. As a result, the adults decided that the door was locked and they were locked in the room! Young children, on the other hand, who had not yet made the generalisation about the doorknob, simply walked up to the door and pushed on it and exited the room. The adults, because of their decisions, created a reality of being locked in the room when in fact they were not. So how many of your decisions (generalisations) about yourself, your partner, your boss, the way it is at work, leave you "locked in", when others are not stopped by it?

One of our challenges is to discover, those filters I have put in place and how they affect what I see, hear, feel; how I react to others and what I create in my life. Once you become aware of filters that do not serve you, you can choose consciously to modify or remove them.

Internal Representations

Do you remember when you first fell in love, do you remember driving in to work the other morning, and do you remember when you first passed your driving test? How do you remember it? Do you see a picture in your mind, or are there smells or tastes? Were there sounds – perhaps in your mind you can hear a radio? To remember an event, your mind uses pictures, sounds, feelings, tastes, smells and words. These perceptions of your "outside world" are called internal representations and are a function of your filters (i.e. beliefs and values). Your perceptions are what you consider to be "real" or in other words your reality.

If you and I went out for dinner, our internal representations or perception of dinner will most likely be similar and different in some way – depending on what is important to each of us (our filters). Dinner is not very controversial. But what about our views on a conflict, e.g. war or political situation? Given our different backgrounds, we may perceive this very differently with significantly different reactions (behaviours).

Filters

Have you ever gone to see a movie with a friend, sat next to each other, saw exactly the same movie and one of you thought it was the best movie ever and the other thought it was terrible? How could that happen? It is quite simple. You and your friend filtered the information differently (different beliefs, values, decisions, etc.). In other words, you perceived the movie differently and hence behaved differently in your reaction to it.

By the way, who put your filters in place? You did! – Based on what happened in your family as you grew up, the teachings of your church (or absence of church), the beliefs and values in the part of the country where you lived, decisions you made about the world (e.g. a safe place or a dangerous place), etc. If your filters are not creating the results that you desire, you are the only person who can change them. The first step is to become consciously aware of the filters you have and what kind of reality (results) they are creating for you.

Internal Representations and Behaviours

Would you like to see the effect internal representations have on your behaviours? Can you think of a really happy event in your life? Close your eyes and get a picture of it in your mind, bring in any sounds, feelings, tastes and smells. Fully experience the event in your mind. Once you have done that, notice if there were any changes in your physiology. Maybe as a result of these memories (internal representations), you had a smile on your face, or sat up straighter, or maybe breathed deeper. I am sure that your physiology changed in some way. I did not ask you to change your physiology, did I? What this demonstrates is that the pictures, sounds, etc. (internal representations) that you make in your mind, influence your physiology and as a result, your choice of words, the tone of voice you use and the behaviours you manifest.

Now sit up straight, put a big smile on your face, and breathe deeply. While you do that, feel sad. I will bet that you could not feel sad without changing your physiology (e.g. shallow breathing, rounded shoulders, etc.). This illustrates that your physiology influences your internal representations (feeling sad or happy). Next time you are feeling sad or down, what can you do? – Participate in some physical activity (e.g. brisk walk, exercise).

Based on your previous experiences, you filter information about the world around you. The resulting internal representations are how you perceive the world (your reality) and this drives your behaviours, often reinforcing that your perception of the world is "correct".

For me, one of the benefits of discovering the filters I have put in place is how they affect what I see, hear, feel; how I react to others and what I create in my life. Once you become aware of those filters that do not serve you, you can choose consciously to modify or remove them, to help you take control of your life and create a life you want, helping you break negative behaviours, unproductive thoughts and limiting beliefs.

The next chapter focuses on how we can overcome any negative habits in a matter of moments. We can change the habits of a lifetime, negative thoughts and behaviours within moments, just as I have done with many thousands of clients over a number of years; you can overcome your biggest fears, negative thoughts and behaviours.

Chapter 3: Breaking Bad Habits

"Bad habits are easier to abandon today than tomorrow".
Yiddish Proverb

Do you ever find yourself repeating certain types of behaviour over and over again? Once you have repeated the behaviour you think damn I can't believe I did that, I can't believe I have done it again.

All of us have habits, some of them serve us and some of them can be detrimental and self-destructive to ourselves and the people around us. Do you have any habits you would like to change? Are there certain things you do that you are fed up doing, and you have reached the point you want to kick that habit?

Whether it's biting your nails, lighting a cigarette, eating too much chocolate cake, approaching a potential date and you can't get the right words out, or any other form of destructive behaviour, the good news is it is possible to change negative habits very quickly, with a technique we shall go through later in the chapter. So, providing you want to remove an existing habit, it is possible to remove it very quickly.

Once a habitual behaviour has been learned it can be beneficial for positive behaviours e.g. exercising, eating well, or be detrimental causing negative behaviour such as smoking and drinking, sabotaging our relationships, or living with our limitations.

Examples of some positive and negative habits

Keeping yourself in good shape by exercising = good habit. Lighting a cigarette when you're stressed at work = bad habit. Tying shoelaces = good habit.

Driving a car = good habit. Biting your nails = bad habit. Fear of flying = bad habit.

Drinking excessive alcohol = bad habit.

Consciously we can distinguish a good or bad habit; most people know smoking damages their health. And what foods, such as fruit and vegetables, are good for them. However, why is it that people carry on sabotaging their lives by smoking, drinking and feeling negative?

If people are aware something isn't good for them, why don't they change?

Habitual behaviour is typically a way of creating order or structure to day-to-day life. Habitual behaviour is learned and then becomes automatic without the person being consciously aware of doing it. Negative habitual behaviours can be detrimental to physical and mental health, the most common being smoking and drinking. They can last a lifetime and be detrimental to someone's life.

I once worked with a client who was very well known in the public eye, a former well-known model who seemed to be struggling to cope with the withdrawal of fame, which brought her the attention she craved which made her feel loved. Without going into the depths of a character analysis of her, she told me she was an alcoholic.

She had been to Alcoholics Anonymous and checked in to various priories and clinics and it seemed to get a bit better before it got worse.

My first thoughts were about the fact she had a self-destructive habit, and hanging around with other people who had the same self-destructive habit was probably only going to make it worse. I guessed if you had a problem and you hung around other people with the same problem who can't overcome it, it's probably not a good idea, though nevertheless, each to their own. Some people think hanging around a group with the same problems, is a good way to overcome a problem. My thoughts are it might serve a purpose initially in helping someone open up, though if someone's serious about moving forward, they need to associate with people who are in the place they would like to be.

The technique I used with this client to help her overcome her drink problem and clean up her act I will illustrate later in the chapter, so you can use it with any habits you may want to change.

First let's explore the mind

The mind has two parts: the conscious and the subconscious. A useful analogy is an iceberg. The conscious mind is the bit that sticks out of the water. The subconscious mind is the bit hidden away underneath the surface.

The subconscious is where all the things that you have learnt to do without thinking is done.

For instance, when you first drove a car, you had to consciously work out where to put each foot and how to use each new control. As your driving skills developed, you handed more and more control over to your subconscious mind. Now you are so proficient that you can drive, navigate and talk to your passenger all at the same time!

Surprisingly, it is the subconscious that can be in control of our behaviour most of the time. Once you realise that, a lot of things begin to make sense. This is the reason people find it very difficult to stop smoking – they have consciously decided that smoking is bad for their health, costs a fortune, is ruining their complexion, etc.. However, they have not taken into account their subconscious reasons for wanting to carry on smoking. Go back to the iceberg analogy; if the little bit at the top wants to go one way and the huge bit at the bottom wants to go the other way, guess who's going to win?

Consciously we know smoking is bad for you, we know eating too much chocolate makes us put on weight; we know drinking too much alcohol isn't good for you.

So why do we do it?

Once you understand about the role of the subconscious, you can understand where a lot of odd behaviour comes from. People get stuck in a rut because their subconscious doesn't know how to change. People can get disturbing thoughts or feelings because the subconscious thinks that something bad is about to happen.

The conscious mind is only aware of a limited amount of information at any given time, (e.g. try driving, talking on your mobile phone and doing your make-up at the same time). The unconscious mind is aware of everything else, the sound of the cars outside, the breeze blowing through the window, the sound of the TV in the background, your feet landing against the pavement as you walk, the aeroplane flying overhead. The millions of memories we store in our mind from the day we are born, birthdays, scoring that winning goal, your first kiss.

Roles of Conscious/Subconscious Mind

→ The conscious mind does your intellectual thinking; is responsible for your self-talk.

→ Your unconscious mind does your perceiving and feeling.

→ The conscious mind is logical. It likes things to make sense – have a reason.

→ The unconscious mind is intuitive and can make associations of information easily.

→ Your conscious mind is associated with the waking, thinking state.

→ The unconscious mind is associated with the dreaming (including daydreaming), reflecting, meditating and sleeping state.

→ The conscious can voluntarily move parts of your body.

→ The unconscious can involuntarily move parts of your body.

→ Your conscious mind is only aware of the now.

→ Your unconscious mind is unlimited in time and space.
It holds all your memories and future constructs.

Our Behaviour

Because our behaviour is governed by our subconscious mind, think about it, physiologically do we need to tell our fingernails to grow, do we need to tell our hair to grow, our heart to beat, tell ourselves to breathe, when we are hungry, feel like going to bed, do we need to consciously tell ourselves how to make a cup of tea?

We just do it almost like we are on autopilot. SUBCONSCIOUSLY.

Successful people, whether they are top athletes or entrepreneurs, have mastered the power of their conscious and subconscious mind to produce their success. Many of us haven't tapped into the unlimited potential of our minds because we lack the understanding of how our minds actually work. When we decidedly focus our effort on creating unity with the conscious and subconscious minds, we can achieve a greater sense of happiness and success in our lives than we ever thought possible.

That explains why people make conscious decisions at the start of every January to go to the gym and get into the best shape ever only to give up by February; statistics say 90 per cent of people who join a gym give up in the first six months. We have all the right intentions though the subconscious mind steers us away.

In order for behaviour to change and last we must work at a subconscious level, if we are going to give up the cigarettes and stay off them, then we need to change at a subconscious level. How you ask, how can I give up the chocolate, give up smoking, stop biting my nails, stop sabotaging my success?

The New Behaviour Generator is one of NLP's simplest and most powerful patterns for changing behaviour. Use it to:

- ➜ Stop smoking
- ➜ Lose weight
- ➜ Get rid of anger problems
- ➜ Break habits
- ➜ Form healthier habits
- ➜ Increase performance
- ➜ Overcome fears and anxieties
- ➜ Get more confidence

You see, the subconscious mind needs clear directions in a very specific format if it's going to motivate you to do something. Without this "road map", change can be very difficult. With this powerful technique the new behaviour is easy and automatic. Old habits you want to get rid of fall away; new healthy habits you wish to replace them with take their place.

One of the things to bear in mind with this technique is by changing your state of mind, i.e. the state of mind you're in when you eat that chocolate cake, pick up that bottle, miss out on going to the exercise class, you can change your state of mind from a negative one to a more positive one, and in the more positive state of mind, you achieve a more positive outcome.

For example you may link feeling stressed in a certain situation to smoking, so by smoking you are compensating for your feelings, by changing your state of mind from feeling stressed, to feeling empowered, the new state of mind produces a new outcome. So instead of picking up a cigarette, in your new empowered state you do something more positive like eat a piece of fruit.

Here are the steps to the New Behaviour Generator technique to assist you in overcoming negative behaviour and unwanted bad habits. First decide on a behaviour you would like to change and decide on a new behaviour to replace it.

1. **Think of a time you demonstrated that behaviour you would like, or choose a role model** that has the behaviour, skills or abilities that you want for yourself, e.g. confident, motivated, excellent public speaker.

2. **Close your eyes and visualise yourself or that person in action.** Watch it like a movie in your mind.

   See how you or they look, how you or they use their body, how you or they use their posture; how you or they stand, walk, and sit. Pay close attention. Hear how you or they talk, what you or they say, and how you or they say it.

3. **Ask yourself: do you really want to adopt this behaviour to change the old one?** Confirm that it is what you want for yourself.

4. **See yourself as the model or yourself conducting this choice of behaviour.** You have stepped into the role model's place. You are watching yourself do as the model does. You have taken over the role and are acting exactly like your role model. Or imagine reliving a time you did the preferred behaviour.

5. **Do you feel any negativity come up within you when you watch yourself?** Are there any doubts that you are capable of doing as the model does or producing your new behaviour? Go through them one by one and adjust them, or adjust your action in the movie, until you are happy with what you see and hear in this new behaviour. Feel positive and confident in your abilities.

6. **Mentally step inside the picture.** You are now inside your movie image, looking through your own eyes. You are no longer watching yourself. You are doing the new behaviour just as you did it in the past or as the model did it. How does it feel to perform this new behaviour or be this person with these new behaviours? How does your body feel? How is your posture? What do you hear? How does your voice sound to you?

7. **Imagine a future situation where you want to behave this way.** Put yourself there. Look through your own eyes at this situation. You are the star of this movie and behaving in the new way! Is it all working? Do you need to make any adjustments?

8. **Open your eyes and come to the present moment.**

9. **Imagine that you are now the new you with the new behaviour.** Get up and walk around as the new model. Walk the walk and talk the talk as they say. How does it feel?

Building new pathways in the mind is a great way to adopt a new behaviour. One way I like to put it is repatterning an existing negative thought process and replacing it with a more productive level of thinking, even by doing this technique it can be powerful enough to move us forward into a more productive thought process and outcome.

Chapter 4: Realigning Yourself

"Live as if you were to die tomorrow. Learn as if you were to live forever."

Mohandas Gandhi

Who are you really and what do you really want?

If someone was to ask you that question what would your answer be?

Think about how would you explain who you were?

And what would you say if someone asked you what you wanted out of life?

What do a Rolex, a Ferrari and a palatial home have in common beyond the obvious...? Even if you possess them, it doesn't mean you will be happy. Many film stars, famous athletes and others have it all, and still we get the most miserable, embarrassing media reports about them, even to the point of death. Most happiness is not based on possessions, but rather love, passion and value. Sometimes we need to find new balance in our lives, no matter what we have or don't have. If we are able to focus and invest in our passion, doing what we love, what makes us special in the world, what we came here to do, that is when we experience life at its most satisfying and fulfilling.

The key to satisfying human needs is to align with the individual's goals. Aim at accomplishing those goals. Each of us has an identity, or core values. Wake up to who you are. Roll up your sleeves. Get off your backside, go out there and achieve your dreams! Your life.

You truly can make that transformation in an instant. If you keep doing what you're doing for the next 25 years, will you be able to say you're happy at the end?

With so many personal developments books on the market, DVDs, CDs, motivational speakers, conferences and courses, programmes and coaches, so many people seem to have the answers to many of the world's problems, and you look around you, pick up a paper, watch TV, and you could be excused for thinking nothing seems to change. Or you might have friends, family, or maybe yourself who have read all the books, seen all the motivational gurus, you may have felt great, for a few hours later, maybe even a day or two or a week, and then bang, back to where you were.

The change happens for a short while however it doesn't last, just take for example people who go in for cosmetic surgery, they change their shape of their nose, then the size of their lips and the list goes on and they still feel negative about themselves. Or they move to a new area, or find a new job and after a short while they're not happy again. For long-lasting change, we have to work on a deeper level than that; at a level significant enough to make change an imprint, and long lasting.

This chapter helps you to get to the bottom of who you are, and understand your life's purpose, it will help you make changes, or make you realise you're fine as you are. If you're interested in finding your true self and getting to know your true self and others then read on.

When I was working at a football club I used to bring in students from university for work experience who all had aspirations to work in football. Many of the students had an idea of what it would be like to work in football, in their mind they had built an image of rubbing shoulders with some of the top football stars, owning fast cars, living in mansions, dating glamorous women, having loads of money and for a few hours of work a day.

I would take the students on work experience, a week in the life of working in the coaching department of a football club. And by the end of the week, most of the perception of what it was like completely changed. It had given them the idea of what it was really like. Different to their perception they had built up. That said there was occasionally the student who really enjoyed what they did, and pursued a career.

On one particular occasion a student worked with me over a week, and it was a demanding week, as we had lost a couple of games, the mood at the club wasn't great.

The getting up early and finishing late had started to make the student a bit tired. I asked him halfway through the week his thoughts; he said he was enjoying it though it was a bit more demanding than what he thought it would be. However he was in the midst of his final dissertation at university and it was keeping him up till the all hours of the morning, though if he did the hard work now things were sure to get easier in the future.

In his own words he gave me a Muhammad Ali quote in regards to work hard now, things become easier later.

I said sure, so after you finish your university course everything is smooth sailing, as easy as that.

As we finished work at 9pm that night after an 8am start, I dropped the student off at his bus stop; he was looking tired and weary after a long week of helping me with different duties.

Soon came Saturday and it was match day. A huge excitement came with match day, anticipation; after all, it's what we prepared for all week. My student came in to report for his duties looking far from enthusiastic after a long week. As the day progressed the game had gotten under way, and it was nearing the end of the game. We were losing, as a team it didn't go to plan. I asked the student, "Could you fill the ice baths in the changing room so they're ready for the end of the match for the players." He went off to the changing room which had three rooms, players change, cubicles, and a spare room for ice baths.

As we walked into the changing room with the players at the end of the match, after a defeat, the manager was not happy to say the least. Emotions were running high.

There was a silence in the changing room, until we could hear someone trying to get out of the spare room. Amidst the silence the manager flung the door open and at the top of his voice said, "Who in the world is this?" Of course it was the student who had locked himself in the spare room whilst preparing the ice baths.

The student looked to go for the exit, as he left for the exit the manager bellowed no one leave the changing room, and he sat in for the end of match discussion, which was emotionally charged to say the least.

When all had settled down and we were making our way home, I asked the student if all was well. He said fine it had been a good week.

I asked him whether he was going to report for training in the morning, as we had scheduled an extra session on Sunday morning to prepare for Tuesday's game. He said no, he didn't think football was for him, he wanted to get into teaching.

This is when it dawned on me, some people like the idea of doing something, though not the doing. What they think it might bring to their life, and not the purpose, enjoyment and fulfilment. I would go so far to guarantee a David Beckham would still be playing football for a Sunday league team, if he wasn't gracing the field for the greatest teams in the world, or a late Michael Jackson would be singing and dancing and making music in his front living room if he wasn't entertaining millions around the world. Whilst the rewards and trappings of a successful career can be great, and given the opportunity of course most people wouldn't knock it back, the true rewards are the enjoyment, fulfilment and intrinsic gratification of doing something you love, and losing yourself in something you're passionate about that is the greatest reward anyone can have.

An excellent way to realign our lives and identify the exact area we need to work on in our lives is using logical levels; logical levels give us an understanding of ourselves, and other people. They can help to identify the exact area of your life to work on to achieve long-lasting change, align yourself with your goals, and turn your life around in the right direction you want to go. Just imagine a ship at sea leaving one destination for another, with no compass, or a plane flying from one destination to another with no navigation system, you could be searching and seeking this destination all your life and never find it, just drifting in the abyss. Logical levels help you find your path and stay on course.

Before we start with the logical level application to your life, or goals you may have, let's run the concept and its application to gain an understanding of how they work. Follow the sequence below, and map it towards a part or parts of your life, e.g. relationships, your work, a goal you may have.

You can reflect on the answers at the end of the chapter when you have grasped the understanding of the logical levels application.

Time to get a pen and paper out and answer the questions in the tables below.

Six Logical Levels

Level	Questions corresponding to logical levels
Spirituality/Purpose	This can be viewed as your connection to a wider purpose. What is your sense of purpose on a personal level? Why are you here? What is your sense of purpose professionally? Why do you do what you do? What is the meaning of your existence both personally and professionally?
Identity/Mission	Who are you as an individual? Who are you to different people? Who are you professionally? Are you achieving your purpose? How do you think of yourself on a personal level? And professionally? E.g. I am an intelligent person, attractive person, good person?
Beliefs and Values	Why do you do what you do?

Personally? And professionally? What do you believe about yourself personally and professionally? What are your key values personally? And professionally? You may believe you are an excellent public speaker. Or you may value honesty. From a professional perspective, you may value good or excellent client care and/or the best interests of the people you speak to.

Capabilities/Strategies	How do you go about doing things? Personally? And professionally? What are your personal and professional capabilities, skills, strategies or action plans?
Behaviours	What are your behaviours? Personally? Professionally?
Environment	Where? When? With whom? Where, when and with who do you display your behaviours? Personally? Professionally? What are the external influences on you?

Example:

To gain an appreciation of how these logical levels work, assume it is 9pm on a Saturday night and you are with your friends at your regular nightspot (environment).

1. You see someone you're attracted to and want to ask him/her on a date, some possible choices are: you could go

up to the person and introduce yourself. You could do a handstand to gain their attention. You could start shouting and acting silly – with the hope a door person would take you out of the nightclub, so you don't have to ask the person out.

2. **The behaviour** you select depends on your **capabilities/strategies**. If you're confident going up to the person and asking them on a date is certainly a possibility. On the other hand, your strategy may be to do a handstand to attract attention from the person and they might be impressed and approach you. Or you might start screaming and acting silly so the door person will escort you out and you have an excuse for not asking the person out, consciously or unconsciously.

3. **The capability/strategy** you choose will depend on your **beliefs and values**. If you believe that you are an attractive, witty, fun person and have a lot to offer to that person if they went out on a date with you then you would more than likely go up to the person and ask them out. If you felt you were inadequate and a person like that would never go out with a person like you (even without asking them) you may look for the exit strategy. Your **beliefs and values** are determined by your **identity**. If you see yourself as an attractive person, then it is very possible that you would hold the **belief** that you interest the other person in going out with you, or of finding someone suitable to you which will.

4. Your **identity** is dependent on your purpose in life – the impact that you wish to have on your community, etc. contribution, having fun, enjoying yourself.

Logical levels is for long-lasting sustainable change.

Sustainable Change

Making a change at a lower level (e.g. environment – going to a different nightspot) may, but not necessarily, affect an upper level. However, a change at an upper level (e.g. belief) will have a distinct impact on the levels below it, as illustrated in the above example.

Using Logical Levels to Explain/Understand Change

The above leads to a number of interesting explanations/discoveries.

Short-term vs. long-term change: Sometimes people find that attending a seminar, buying a book, seeing a coach, worked great at changing an unwanted behaviour for a short period of time, and eventually the unwanted behaviour returned. How can this be? If the new behaviour was not in alignment with the person's beliefs and values or identity, the higher level would override the lower level.

For change at the behaviour level to be long-term, the desired behaviour change must either be in alignment with the higher levels or the change must take place at a high level e.g. identity.

Making changes:

Have you ever made some changes?

Bought a new sports car? Purchased some new clothes? Started socialising in a different area? This is change at the level of environment. Do you think it will be long-lasting? Only if the change is in alignment with the higher levels.

Or maybe you start going to the gym and get in tip-top shape **(behaviour)**, learn some dating techniques to approach the people **(capability/strategy)**, though still change doesn't last, you may feel better about yourself for a short period of time, though you go back to how you perceived yourself before.

Health/Career: Suppose you have a goal for yourself (health, career), and it is not in alignment with one of the higher levels. How successful do you think you will be in achieving your goal? For example, I know many people who like the idea of doing things, as we discussed earlier in the chapter, though actually doing it is not what they want, i.e. they like the idea of being a pop star because they think it will bring them fame and fortune, though they don't like the idea of working hard, going on tour, learning to play an instrument, working on their singing, or starting out playing to potential audiences of a few people.

"The problems of today can only be solved at a higher level of thinking than that which created them." – Albert Einstein

I have heard many people refer to this quote yet few can explain how you can actually do it (i.e. move to a higher level of thinking). Using logical levels, you can easily explain it. For example, if there is a problem at the behavioural level, to solve it we must move to at least the capability/strategy level.

NLP can assist you in making change at the higher levels (beliefs and values, identity, and spirituality/purpose) or can help you to ensure that your goals are aligned at all levels. Once this happens, your goals in life often become clear and obtained effortlessly.

Spirituality/Purpose, Identity/Mission, Beliefs and Values, Capabilities/Strategies, Behaviours, and Environment. In this chapter, we present other ways to look at the logical levels and an exercise to assist you with achieving personal congruence – all of the levels are in alignment.

Getting to Know another Person through logical levels

If you really want to get to know another person

You can only observe two of the logical levels of another person – behaviour and environment. You can observe what they are doing and when, where and with whom. This will give you some idea as to their capabilities/strategies, beliefs and values, etc.

To really be sure, you need to engage them in a conversation on these subjects. Having conversations with another person at the higher logical levels provides you with a more intimate understanding of that person and why they behave the way they do. How often do you have a conversation with someone you really care about and the topic is the weather (environment) or what they are doing (behaviour) rather than who they see themselves being (identity/mission) or what are their beliefs and values? And to engage in this type of conversation, you need to create a space where each of you feels safe in disclosing your "inner selves".

Using logical levels to identify where conflicts exist professionally or personally:

➜ How many people take a job only to realise they are not suitable, it's not what they want to do, it's not for them?

➜ How many organisations have deep divisions between management and staff?

➜ How many of the world's problems and conflicts exist because of misalignment of the higher logical levels?

A number of years ago, I conducted a study as to why a certain fitness organisation was not retaining its staff and client members. Their policy was to attract new members and as many as possible and in doing that, they were neglecting customer care of existing members, the equipment wasn't being maintained, the showers weren't being cleaned as often as they should, facilities were being run down. Discounts were being offered for new people to join the gym though not existing members. The gym staff were not being sent on training courses to increase their knowledge. The gym staff were also asked to work longer hours and spend less time looking after members, e.g. writing training programmes, health checks were abolished, the ethos of the organisation had changed.

As you may expect, most of the fitness staff had difficulty with the changes. Staff and members were leaving the organisation. Before proceeding, let's have a look at this situation through the lens of the NLP Logical Levels.

Health and Fitness staff:

Spirituality/Purpose (connection to a larger system): Make a significant contribution to the community of people who require assistance and support to get in good shape and improve well-being.

Identity/Mission: Well-trained fitness professionals that can assist people to get in good shape and increase well-being.

Beliefs and Values: He/she has the fitness skills and abilities to assist others. Another important belief held by many of the fitness staff is that they think it's important they write fitness programmes for members, monitor programmes and do health checks rather than spend time doing other duties such as admin and sales, (the fitness staff said they didn't go into the industry to spend a high proportion of time doing sales and administration).

Capabilities/Strategies: Many positive capabilities/strategies for designing fitness programmes, health checks. Less than supportive (in some cases dysfunctional) capabilities/strategies for administration and sales.

Behaviours: The behaviours of a competent, confident, motivated, fitness professional when working in a gym environment. Distressed behaviours when asked to perform in a "sales environment" – in some cases, fed up and feeling like walking out.

Environment: Gym fitness or a sales environment.

From a logical levels point of view, can you see why staff and member retention was a problem?

You had an organisation driven to get as many paying new members on board as possible, neglecting existing members who also paid, somewhere along the way, the organisation had lost its key priority and focus, on providing a service their staff could be proud to offer their members.

Which conflicts with some excellent key members of staff at a higher logical level? (Keeping a paying member is as good as attracting a new member.)

Could you use a similar approach with your family, your staff or co-workers that would allow them to see the situation differently and to draw on their strengths to overcome a perceived obstacle?

Aligning Logical Levels for Personal Congruence

For many of us, the logical levels operate outside of our conscious awareness. Whether we are aware of them or not, they have a significant influence over the quality of our lives.

The following exercise will help you to:

1. Become consciously aware of what factors influence how you live your life.

2. Identify possible conflicts.

3. Recognise possible changes you can make to bring the levels more in alignment and hence achieve a higher level of personal congruence (reduced inner conflict).

I suggest you take your time doing this exercise and write down your answers.

Spirituality/Purpose: For the larger system (e.g. family, co-workers, people needing your service/product, community,) what is your purpose or the impact you wish to have?

Identity/Mission: Who are you or what role do you play? Is it the role necessary to achieve your purpose? What do you need to change?

Beliefs and Values: What beliefs do you have about yourself, about others, about the world in general? Do these beliefs support you in fulfilling your role? What do you value in yourself, others, the world in general? Are these values in alignment with your role? Are there other beliefs and values that you could take on that would be more in alignment?

Capabilities/Strategies: What capabilities/strategies/action plans do you have? Do you need to develop new capabilities, strategies or action plans? Are they in alignment with each of the above logical levels? If not, what needs to be changed? Maybe you need to change your capabilities (get more training), your strategies or action plans. Or maybe, given this new information, you need to reassess your purpose, your role or your beliefs and values.

Behaviours: What do people really see/experience in your behaviours? Are your behaviours in alignment with each of the above logical levels? Does something need to be changed?

Environment: When, where, with whom do you do these behaviours? Are they in alignment with the above logical levels?

Aligning Your Goals with Your Logical Levels

Many of our goals (career, family, romance, health, purpose in life) are based on the requests, desires or expectations of others – parents, spouse, teachers, religious leaders, boss or society. These are not our goals and hence we do not have the energy that propels us forward to truly achieve our goals. When we struggle with our goals, almost always there is some hidden inner conflict that must be resolved. Often we are less than fully alive because of these inner conflicts. The following exercise will assist you in identifying these conflicts and realigning your goal with who you really are. Think about your goal and answer the same questions for the logical levels as you did above. Notice if there is an alignment between the answers. For example you may find that achieving your goal would take time away from being with your spouse and children (assuming this is an important value for you). If this is the case, is there some way to adjust your goal or your strategies/action plan to spend time with your family and still achieve your goal? You may wish to ask those affected by your goal, as they often come up with solutions that you would never think of.

This process will allow you to become aware of the alignment (or lack of it) between your inner self and your goals. As you fine-tune your goals and align them with your inner self, you should find that your goals become clearer, more compelling and more easily achieved. You have a stronger sense of fulfilment and understanding of your life.

Chapter 5: Dare to Dream

Living a Dream

"Many of us crucify ourselves between two thieves - regret for the past and fear of the future."

Fulton Oursler

If I Had My Life to Live Over

I once came across a poem called *If I Had My Life to Live Over* written by an 85-year-old woman. In it she talks of all the things she would do if she had a second chance and it ends:

I would go barefoot earlier in the spring and stay that way later in the fall.

I would go to more dances.

I would ride more merry-go-rounds. I would pick more daisies.

Regret can describe not only the dislike for an action that has been committed, but also, importantly, regret of inaction. Many people find themselves wishing that they had done something in a past situation. Most people regret the things they haven't done, not the things they have.

As a child did you ever have a dream, what did you want to be and do? Playing the guitar to a packed audience at a music festival?

Did you ever imagine kicking the winning goal at Wembley Stadium in front of 80,000 cheering fans? Or singing in front of 100,000, writing an amazing best-selling novel, being an astronaut?

As a child you may have mentioned your dream to one of your teachers, parents, family or friends. You were told you weren't good enough, clever enough, or talented enough. It's not for you, and before you know it ten years has gone by in your life, your circumstances change, the goalposts completely move and your focus moves towards other things in life, paying the lousy bills, getting up in the morning and doing a job you can't stand just to get by, and you find yourself thinking is this it?

As time passes you by, circumstances change and the dreams you once had get locked away in the cupboard. You're almost resigned to any possibilities, seeing out time till you get your pension, then you can retire and unwind and kick back, maybe retire somewhere relaxing with a slow pace of life, kids have all grown up, you can just kick back and take things at your own pace. Everything completely mapped out, though the strange thing is you haven't mapped any of it out, it has all been mapped out for you, by whom?

Stop and think about it for a minute, is this what you have envisaged for your life?

If you were approaching the end of your life, what would you be thinking?

Take a few minutes to write down your thoughts.

Have you ever wondered what it would be like to:

+ Go travelling around the world
+ See the Pyramids
+ See all the Seven Wonders of the World
+ Swim with dolphins
+ Go tracking in Africa

- Get into the best shape ever
- Run a successful business
- Write a romantic novel
- Learn to speak another language
- Learn to dance
- Go into a children's hospital ward and give out some toys
- Raise some funds for a charity
- Go into an old person's home at Christmas and listen to someone's life story
- Or maybe you have done some of the things mentioned above or maybe even all of them and you're looking forward to some other amazing experiences in your life

What are some of the dreams you once had though and put away?

Life is short and you owe it to yourself. Every dream starts with a vision.

Did you ever have a dream or have a vision?

What are you passionate about, what do you enjoy so much that you would pay to do?

Do you have a dream?

I once read a story about a woman who started writing a book whilst she was stuck on a delayed train between Manchester and London, it was 1990. Shortly after she moved abroad to teach in Portugal, however after a brief marriage in Portugal and now with a baby, she returned to Britain in 1993, settling in Edinburgh, Scotland, to be near her sister. She suffered through a period of poverty and depression while she struggled to earn a living and take care of her daughter. It was during this difficult time that she finally completed her book. The book was about a boy called

Harry – a lonely, downtrodden 11-year-old orphan who learns he is actually a wizard when he is magically invited to attend Hogwarts School of Witchcraft and Wizardry. Following its publication in Britain in June 1997, the book quickly became a hit, won numerous awards, including the British Book Awards' Children's Book of the Year, J.K Rowling received an OBE (Order of the British Empire), a medal of achievement awarded by the Queen, in March 2001 and has gone on to become no doubt one of the most successful writers of all time.

Many things we take for granted now, much of the technology we use all started as a dream, a vision in someone's mind, films we watch, songs we listen to, the cars we drive, phones we use, planes we fly, books we read, they were all at some point just someone's dream. Walt Disney, the Wright brothers, and Henry Ford, the list goes on, all started with a dream.

Young Albert Einstein for example; while still an awkward adolescent headed for a boring job at the patent office, he dreamed a dream that changed the course of human history – for better or worse. He reported this dream, the precursor to his Theory of Relativity, in an interview with famed journalist, Edwin Newman.

Einstein told Newman that it was night in the dream and he was with friends sledding down a hill and having a grand time. However on one trip down, he became aware that he was travelling faster and faster. Realising after a moment that the sled was approaching the speed of light, he looked up and saw the twinkling starry light of the night refracted into a brilliant spectrum of colours he had never before seen. Filled with a numinous sense of awe, wonder and reverence, he intuitively understood he was witnessing an event that contained his calling in life – all the answers as well as questions he would need to ask. "I knew I had to understand that dream," he told Newman, "and you could say and I would say, that my entire scientific career has been a meditation on that dream."

All things are possible if we dare to dream, we have the most amazing powerful resources at our disposal, the human mind.

We are all wired up with the same resources within our mind; it's how we use those resources which make the difference.

Some people dream big and go for it; some people decide to dream within the realms of what they perceive as reality. It never ceases to amaze me what is possible when we let our mind just wander and flow.

The following exercise is developed by eliciting from some of the greatest dreamers of the last century, people like Walt Disney, who had the most amazing strategy to come up with the most amazing ideas.

By using the same strategies with your mind, let your mind wander knowing you don't have to tie yourself into anything you don't want to follow up. Though rest assured that every positive thought we have will reward us in some way.

Turning a vision into a dream a dream into reality exercise

Exercise

Write down as many things as possible, if time or money were no object, you would like to achieve.

Step 1:

Think of a time when you were really creative, when you were making some very creative choices. Fully associate to a time you were really creative and relive that time. What did it feel like, what did you see, colours, images, what could you hear? Let yourself go completely. It might have been a time you were on a beach relaxing, going for a country walk, having a meal with family and friends, listening to some music. Let your mind run free, relax and go into its creative state. Close your eyes really relax and let your mind wander.

In your creative state

Now think about your life's purpose, what are you here for? What are you passionate about?

If you could do anything what would it be?

If money and time were no object what would you like to do?

Imagine living in a world with no limitations, even for a few minutes, have some fun.

Step 2:

Think of a time when you were realistic about some plan and put it into action in an effective way. It might be your own plan or somebody else's. An idea you had which you put into action, it could have been completing a course, setting up a business, going travelling. As you recall this time relive the experience. Think about what you saw, what it felt like, what you heard, gather and recollect some of your thoughts and actions of a time you had an idea which you put in practise and relive the situation.

In your realistic state of mind

Come up with some logistics for your plan.

What are some of the resources you would require for your plan, if you were to implement it e.g. resources?

Planning? Time? Investment?

Step 3:
Think of a time when you criticised a plan in a constructive way and saw weaknesses as well as strengths and identified problems. Again it might be your plan or someone else's. As you recall this time relive the experience, think of the images you saw, the feelings you had, what you heard, now gathering your thoughts reflect and recollect your actions.

In your critical mindset
Come up with potential pitfalls of the dream e.g. cost? Time?

Step 4:
Now think again of a time when you were really creative, when you were making some very creative choices. Fully associate to a time you were really creative and relive that time. What did it feel like, what did you see, colours, images, what could you hear? Let yourself go completely. It might have been a time you were on a beach relaxing, going for a country walk, having a meal with family and friends, listening to some music. Let your mind run free, relax and go into its creative state.

Really relax and let your mind wander, and as you let your mind wander notice what you learnt from a time you planned an idea and implemented it and a time you criticised an idea and think about what you have learned. Now reflecting and processing your thoughts, what are some ideas and plans you would like to live?

Exercise

What dream or dreams do you have that you're a ready to take out of your cupboard drawer again or have sprung to mind?

Be excited, get excited and passionate knowing you have awoken your mind again.

Remember it's never too late and there is no better time than the present.

A dream is only fantasy unless you take action. How do you take action?

In the next chapter we will design our destiny and turn your dreams into a reality.

Chapter 6: Setting Goals and Staying Motivated

"If you don't design your own life plan, chances are you'll fall into someone else's plan. And guess what they have planned for you? Not much."

Jim Rohn

How many people moan about aspects of their life, not having a partner or the ideal partner, not having enough money, being overweight, not enjoying their job, they are bored, fed up, disillusioned? Though they keep walking on the treadmill of life, never doing anything about their circumstances, just leaving things to chance, waking up in the morning and whatever will be will be. Neither here nor there, fitting in to a routine of plodding along, going to a job they don't enjoy or don't find the least bit rewarding or coming home to watch TV to fill in the gaps. Drifting along not making the most of their potential, just living in silent desperation hoping someday some miracle will happen, they might win the lottery; meet their knight in shining armour, or princess, leaving their life to chance.

How many people take the time to sit down and think about how they want to live their lives, how they want their life to go, what they want out of life, places they would like to go, things they would like to achieve, people they would like to meet, things they would like to learn?

I consider myself lucky to have worked with thousands of people over many years across a broad range of areas, business, sport, personal development, and I would have to say only very few of them, prior to working with myself, actually sat down and consciously designed their own destiny and set goals; possibly around 10%, and they seemed to be the ones who had a stronger sense of fulfilment and purpose in their lives, living life the way they wanted to. I have come across many people in life who say they don't set goals; they just live and take things as they come. Well at least they might not consciously set goals, though as long as you're alive whether you realise it or not you have adopted a goal-setting strategy. If you're getting up for work in the morning, going to a boring job you don't like, or you're not working and picking up a pay cheque, you still have a goal. Whether it's to pay the lousy bills, or the damned mortgage, they are still goals. Or maybe you're part of someone else's goals, you're paying that damn car off, didn't the sales person see you coming. You see whether you realise it or not goals are a fundamental part of life. The two choices you have are either you carry on leaving things to chance, or you take control of your life living in a way that brings you fulfilment, purpose and happiness.

I guess with setting goals comes the fear of not achieving them, which is understandable; imagine setting these awesome goals only to fall flat on your face and not achieve them, what then? Well I think the most amazing thing about setting goals, is the journey and sometimes we don't achieve what we set out to achieve. We achieve something more significant, and more often than not, in the process of working towards and achieving goals, so many other possibilities are opened and in our life we achieve so much more than we set out to achieve.

I was asked by the producer of BBC GMR radio about a potential series about helping someone overcome barriers. We discussed at length suitable applicants considering much of my work at the time was in sport. The potential candidates for the series revolved around people in a variety of situations, wanting to lose weight, start a new career, find a partner, overcome phobias, the list went on. So I left it to the producer to find someone for the series. I received a call from the producer saying they had found someone. I was excited at the prospect of working with someone, helping them fulfil their potential. I paused for a few seconds and thought I wonder who it is going to be?

The producer told me her name is Margaret she's 65 years of age; she is looking to lose weight and isn't training at present.

A meeting was arranged with Margaret and myself. Prior to the meeting I was excited by the prospect of working with her. After all I had been working mainly in sport for a few years preceding that so I felt this would present a completely different challenge. How easy would it be to help someone lose weight? I had been working with some of the best athletes and football teams in the country, helping someone lose weight and get in great shape would be a completely new challenge.

Finally the day arrived where I met Margaret and she came across as a real amazing person, and I know this statement is used regularly, though in some ways she seemed to have the steely determination to turn things around almost like my athletes had. First of all we had a bit of a chat and I did what I tell all my clients, if I had a magic wand and you could achieve anything you wanted to what it would be? And so the story went, we sat down, set a few goals and decided to see were the road would take us. The next few months would be the most amazing journey, we would report back regularly to the radio station and update on how we were getting on.

Margaret was very specific about what she wanted to achieve, she knew exactly what weight she wanted to be, dress size etc.

The journey began, Margaret had joined different exercise classes ranging from aerobics to t'ai chi, she had completely changed what she was eating and each time I saw her she was getting in better shape, to the point we set up an exercise class on Saturday mornings. On one occasion I saw her running with Sara, and I couldn't believe it as she told me she hadn't run for over 20 years due to arthritis.

The changes she was making were outstanding; in one of our last sessions as the series was drawing to close, she told me there was something she had always wanted to do. She had booked a holiday to Spain, she wanted to be able to swim, I said that's easy enough just take lessons. She explained she had a phobia of swimming pools that she had had since she was eight years of age, and she had tried everything to get rid of it, though it was still there.

She asked me if NLP and hypnotherapy could help her remove it. I said sure after all we had come so far, we could go the extra mile. And it would be a fantastic way to conclude the series.

So I explained to the producer of the show what we were going to do and she said great.

I did what we call in NLP the fast phobia cure and timeline, a couple of techniques I will go into a bit later in the book. I worked with Margaret on a Monday night and she had booked in a swimming lesson on a Wednesday. We had our final show scheduled on the Friday. Margaret phoned me on Wednesday and she said I am really sorry I could not go in the swimming pool. I said that's fine tell me what happened, she said her friend had phoned her on the way to the pool and said are you sure you want to do this? After all do you really believe all this stuff? And that was that, she decided to turn back.

I said to Margaret we go again, let's book it again next Wednesday and keep booking it till we get there.

By the way, the radio show on the Friday had been cancelled so all the listeners waiting to see what happened had to wait another week and it was worth the wait.

It was the following Wednesday afternoon and I could tell from the excitement in Margaret's voice she had done it, she had gone in the pool for the first time in around 56 years and loved it, and booked a whole course of lessons.

The final show on Friday we recapped everything and realised this was an amazing journey. Margaret was in the best shape she had ever been, was participating in a number of different exercise classes and was back swimming after 56 years.

In the process of setting one goal Margaret had gone on to achieve more than we could ever have imagined, not bad for someone who was told by the medical profession her thyroid problem would make it medicinally difficult for her to lose weight. Had Margaret never embarked on her first goal of losing weight so many things which in the broad scheme of things were probably more significant to her would never have been achieved. Overcoming her phobia, which gave her the opportunity to go swimming and socialise with her friends, amongst many other things that may have not been part of the plan initially, though once we shifted our focus into a positive direction, all things were possible.

Goal setting is a powerful process for thinking about your ideal future, and for motivating yourself to turn this vision of the future into reality. Goal setting techniques are used by top-level athletes, successful business people and achievers in all fields. Goal setting gives you long-term vision and short-term motivation. Goal setting focuses your acquisition of knowledge and helps you to organise your time and your resources so that you can make the very most of your life. I believe it is important to set goals for different parts of your life.

Some people are successful in certain parts of their lives and struggle in different areas. It is possible to focus too much on one area of your life and neglect other areas. For example you may spend a huge proportion of your life building a business and neglecting your family, and come home one day and find your family life is completely breaking down.

To create a life of fulfilment, growth and purpose, a life that's balanced, it is important to set goals in different areas of our life.

I remember working with a successful business person once who was a master of setting business goals, though amongst the success he was experiencing professionally, his marriage was breaking up. He said it was the most successful he had been in his life business wise though it was also the emptiest he had been in many years. I asked him in light of his personal circumstances and knowing how much priority he placed on business, how much time are you spending with you wife and children, what plans have you made with them? His response was he wasn't in the business of setting goals were his family was concerned, that was something he did with business. Well I don't personally profess to be a marriage counsellor or expert, though one thing I know for sure is if you're spending 12 to 14 hours a day consistently working Monday to Friday and on weekends playing golf and watching football and spending very little time with your family the balance is disproportionate. And if it means consciously sitting down, and making sure you prioritise for something that is the most important thing in your life, and other things that are important, then energy must be focused in that area because if things are left to chance we never know what we are going to get; you wouldn't gamble your family at a roulette table.

Before we begin the exercises to assist you in setting powerful goals let's look at Maslow's hierarchy of needs which is a theory in psychology, proposed by Abraham Maslow in his 1943 paper *A Theory of Human Motivation*. What we are working towards as people for fulfilment and happiness are our basic needs. These are biological and basic life needs such as food, shelter, warmth, rest and sleep, beyond that we need stability and security, a need to belong, to be loved, our esteem needs a sense of achievement, personal growth, self actualisation and enlightenment.

The following are **exercises** where you can list the things you want for different aspects of your life.

After you have listed your goals, we will then utilise a powerful technique to achieving your goals.

The goal setting is based on you continuing to develop key aspects of all your life, just as the famous psychologist Maslow who developed the hierarchy of human needs suggested, we needed fulfilment in different areas of our life.

If we were to flourish in one area of our lives and completely focus on one area and neglect other areas what would happen?

What happens to the people that work 12 hours a day 7 days a week, regardless of how much money they make?

What happens to the people who are forever chasing the dream of fame and fortune then have all the money you could imagine and are on the front cover of every magazine, and on TV every night, then they profess to not being happy, even depressed, disillusioned, and eventually turn to substances to enhance their feelings? What are we all searching for, what do we all really want out of life?

I have adapted the model to the modern-day environment as times are different to the 1940s when it was developed; however basic needs have always been and will always be the same.

Exercise

Though before we begin the goal setting strategy...

Create Your Vision Board

Get a piece of poster board and attach it to a wall in your office or home where you will see it often. As you go through magazines, brochures, etc. and you see pictures of the things you want, cut them out and glue them to your vision board. In other words, make yourself a collage of the goals that excite you... knowing full well that as you look at them every day, they will soon be yours.

E.g. cut out a picture of the house you want, the car, the places you want to travel to.

Now complete the following exercise:

Write one goal you have for each of the following categories, you may think of others, though for now write one goal you have in each category.

Personal Goals

What would you like to achieve for yourself? Travel? Swimming with dolphins? Watch a cup final live? Go see your favourite musician? Learn to fly?

Characteristics

Is any part of your mindset holding you back, e.g. self-belief, self-esteem, confidence? Is there any part of the way that you behave that upsets you? If so, set a goal to improve your behaviour or find a solution to the problem.

Career

What are you passionate about? What do you enjoy doing, something you have always wanted to do?

Education

What do you want to learn, go back and finish your high school education, learn how to sing, dance, get a degree, learn some new skills?

Family

How is your relationship with your family? How would you like it to be?

Financial

How much money do you want to earn each week? Month? Every year?

Physical

Is there an ideal weight you want to be? Run a marathon? Fun run?

Pleasure

How do you want to enjoy yourself? – You should ensure that some of your life is for you!

Spiritual/Contribution

Do you want to make the world a better place? If so, how?

Now choose one of the goals from the above categories.

(You can use the following strategy for all the goals you have listed above, and incorporate it into to your planning, though for now choose one.)

A common question many people ask is can I set more than one goal? Of course you can, you can set as many goals as you want, particularly for different aspects of your life to ensure growth. However, I would suggest using the strategy and the following exercise for one goal till you develop your action plan, then you can set a different action plan for different goals.

Using the following powerful strategy you can take a goal you have listed in the above category to put into action.

Goal Setting

1. State the goal in positive terms

What do you want to achieve, what would you like to happen, what outcome do you want?

Remember the mind cannot process a negative instruction, for example if I say don't think of the colour red, what comes to mind?

So be specific, if a 5-year-old can't understand it, it's too complex, (for example, in the context of health and fitness, stating you want to lose weight, is vague and not specific. Write your ideal weight you want to be e.g. 12 stone or dress size ten, or the exact car you want, type of partner, business) be as specific as possible. State it in the positive (what you want to achieve).

Where are you now?

This is your road map in the context of your goal (e.g. just starting up in business, 15 stone, never completed a fun run).

Where do you want to be?

Where do you want to be in the case of your goal? What outcome do you want?

(A successful business seeing 20 clients per week charging the market rate per session, 12 stone, complete 5-mile fun run.)

2. Specify the goal in sensory based terms

Remember we learn through our senses, and build an association through our senses which makes it real.

Engage all of your senses in this description process to employ more of your brain and nervous system and build pathways in your mind making it real.

What will you see, hear, feel, etc., when you have achieved your goal?

Close your eyes and imagine what it would be like having achieved your goal, what will you see? Hear? And feel? What steps or stages are involved in reaching this goal?

Formulate a plan. What steps are necessary in achieving the goal? (Step 1: 2: 3: and so forth.)

(E.g. Step one might be to email or phone someone. Step two, set up a business meeting. Step three, identify your strengths and weaknesses.)

3. Specify the goal in a way that you find compelling

(Make the goal have meaning, specify your goal in a meaningful way.)

Now imagine in your mind's eye the steps you have mapped taking you to the point of having achieved your goal. See yourself having achieved your goal like watching yourself on TV. Notice the screen the clarity of the image, what you are wearing, what people around you are wearing, the surroundings, what you are saying, what the people around you are saying and what it feels like to see yourself achieve the goal. What would achieving the goal mean to you? To your family?

What impact will it have on the greater community?

Is the goal compelling? Does it make you excited?

4. **Run an ecology check on your goal (the consequences of working towards your goal or achieving it) to make sure it is for you in all areas of your life. Making sure it's what you want for you.**

→ Is the desired goal right for you in all circumstances of your life?

→ Is your goal appropriate in all your personal relationships?

→ What will having your goal give you that you do not now have? What implications does it have on other parts of your life e.g. spending time with your children, your partner, family?

→ Is your goal achievable?

5. **The plan**

→ Where, when, how, with whom, etc. will you get this goal?

Where? (E.g. office in city centre celebrating grand opening, running New York Marathon.)

When? Set a time limit, e.g. set an exact date, (by 12/10/2012 successful business seeing 20 clients per week at top market rate,) set a date and even a time for when you will achieve your goal.

How? How you intend to achieve your goal step by step, (generate a plan, set up website, business cards, meeting with key people, join the gym, hire personal trainer).

Whom? List of the resources, as in people that can help you achieve your goal, (family, friends, business manager).

6. **State the resources needed to achieve the goal**

→ What resources will you need in order to get this goal?

- Who will you have to become?
- Who else has achieved this goal?
- Have you ever had or done this before?
- Do you know anyone who has?
- What prevents you from moving toward it and attaining it now?

7. Evidence procedure

- How will you know that your goal has been realised?

(How many times do we achieve a goal without even realising it? It's important to know when you have realised your goal; you wouldn't climb the highest mountain and not sit and admire the view.)

What will let you know that you have attained that desired state?

(How will it feel when you have achieved your goal? How many people achieve a goal and think is that it, or are not sure if they're getting closer, identify the feelings that will come with achieving your goal, close your eyes and think about what feeling you will have, having achieved your goal.)

Placing goals on a timeline

Placing your goal in a timeline gives you the opportunity to note the progress you are making step by step.

Starting with the end in mind, at the very top write specifically what your goal is and the exact date you will achieve it.

E.g. July 2012 dress size 10, weight ten stone, or give up job, go full-time business seeing 20 clients per week, making top market rate with each client.

March 2012 dress size 12, see 10 clients per week part-time.

Jan 2012 dress size 14, see 5 clients per week part-time. December 2011 complete 5-mile fun run, or go part-time at work.

August 2011, enter 5-mile fun run, or start building website, marketing plan.

June 2011,hire personal trainer, do one session per week and two on my own, or set up meeting with business manager with an eye to accumulate enough funds to go full-time in business.

The following exercise brings a sense of reality to achieving your goals and makes them manageable:

After the exercise there is a chart you can use to break your goals down in a time frame.

1. Write down what you envision for yourself in 10 years time. Write down your goals in list form using complete sentences. Use adjectives and be specific. Instead of writing, "running a business," write, "I run a successful business employing ten staff selling a product enhancing the lives of others."

2. Create tasks for each goal. Assign each task a due date, step 1, 2, 3 and so forth. Begin each task with an action verb. Instead of writing, "language classes," write, "Enrol in a "specific" language class (e.g. French, Italian) at the local college."

3. Write down what you envision for yourself in one year as a milestone to know you're on track. Use your list of 10 year goals as a template.

4. Create tasks for each one-year goal. Use your list of tasks for your 10 year goals as a template. Assign each goal at least one task per week.

5. Place your lists in a visible location. Put your lists on your bedroom wall or somewhere else that you look at daily.

6. Write your goals and tasks on a calendar. Put the tasks on their corresponding due dates. Write the goals on to estimated dates or dates of completion.

7. Use the lists and calendar as a template for one-week tasks, one-month goals, 10-year goals and other time frames.

   See the below outline to achieving your goals, what you aim to achieve in specific time frames.

   Write down where you want to be in relation to achieving your goal at each time frame.

10 years

5 years

3 years

2 years

1 year

6 months

3 months

1 month

List your long-term, medium-term, and short-term goals in here and write the milestones along the way.

Weekly Planner

Action plans are essential if you're going to get the most out of your time.

Weekly planning helps you to: decide how to make effective use of your time.

Work proactively rather than reactively.

Write down your daily tasks taking you closer to achieving your goals.

Time	Monday	Tuesday	Wednesday	Thursday	Friday	Saturday	Sunday
6am to 7am	Task 1,2,3 (phone, email etc…)						
7am to 8am							
8am to 9am							
9am to 10am							

10am to 11am						
11am to 12pm						
12pm to 1pm						
1pm to 2pm						
2pm to 3pm						
3pm to 4pm						
4pm to 5pm						
5pm to 6pm						

6pm to 7pm							
7pm to 8pm							

How to Stay Motivated

Most people will agree that motivation plays a big role in your ability to achieve anything.

How many people start with the intention of getting in the best shape ever in the new year, make getting into shape one of their new year resolutions, join a gym, only to give up a few weeks later? Or come up with some fantastic ideas for a new business; decide they want to embark on a journey to travel the world? Get into training for a fun run, enrol on a new course at college, or university, and give up a few weeks later, or halfway through?

I am sure you have come across people who have committed themselves on some level to do at least one of the above ideas, possibly even all of them, or maybe you may have given something a go yourself, and as soon as things got a bit tough, given up. Or you found your motivation disappeared.

Or there may have been a point in your life where you were prompted into action and you kept the momentum going, you sustained your action. You found the motivation to give up drinking excessive alcohol after overdoing it one night and as a result, losing control and doing something stupid. Or the motivation to give up smoking after a trip to your doctor telling you, you have got to the point if you carry on smoking a year from now you could die from a lung-related illness. Not having the energy to play sports with your children because of carrying excess weight, you make a decision to lose weight, shed those extra pounds once and for all. Going in to work and being given orders by the new boss half your age, prompts you to start a new business. Sometimes we are prompted into action by circumstances and events in our life.

Faced with the prospect of consequences ignites us into action, to the point where the consequences are so powerful we continue the momentum. We don't need to wait until we are prompted to react by circumstances and events in our life, you can be in the box seat, you can do the running, it's great having goals though if you don't have the motivation, you don't have the fuel burning the fire.

Motivation Keeps the Flame Burning

You can be motivated and stay motivated to achieve your aspirations in life.

We all have it within us to be motivated and stay motivated, later on in the chapter we have a powerful strategy to help you ignite your motivation and keep it going.

For now let's explore:

What motivates you?

Why do you do the things you do?

Give one reason as to why you work?

Go to the gym? Socialize? Travel?

Read books?

Play sport?

With everything we do in life there must be a degree of motivation or we wouldn't do it.

In my experience of working with some of the most highly motivated athletes and business people, they all have strong enough reasons (motive) for doing what they do. The drive to compete, train, work, push themselves to the limit. I have also had the opportunity to work with groups of people who are in a time in their life where they lack motivation to work, learn, study, and have resigned themselves from certain aspects of life. They still have an element or degree of motivation otherwise they would do nothing at all, at some point they will wake up in the morning and get out of bed and eat, watch television, or some form of activity. This is a degree of motivation in itself. Research has proven that the ingredients to motivation are the same whether the task is to get out of bed in the morning or to go for a run at 6am. Regardless of the desired outcome the same forces of motivation either away from things or toward them, are continually at work. One thing that has always fascinated me is what drives people on to live their lives in a certain way. We all have a choice, we can all decide how we want to live our lives, and underneath those choices people's lives are shaped.

What is Motivation?

Motivation is the level of drive we feel to perform certain tasks at a given time. It is a mysterious thing because although a simple concept, the science of motivation can be rather complex. What drives one person is different to what drives another and yet at its core, what drives each of us is the same.

Through understanding motivation and how it affects our behaviour on a daily basis we can harness powerful forces to aid in the pursuit of our goals. Without continual motivation of the right kind, there can be no success.

Some Thoughts

We all have things which motivate us, which vary from context to context.

We are motivated either to move "Towards" things, (pleasure) or "Away From" things, (pain) or a combination of the two. This is similar to the "carrot or stick".

Think of the reason you gave earlier in the chapter as to what motivated you to do certain tasks.

<u>We are motivated away from pain or towards pleasure.</u>

Example

Why do some people exercise?

Either because they want to give themselves a better chance of avoiding the negative health consequences of not keeping fit (away from pain), or have that amazing six-pack to show off at the beach (towards pleasure). Some people might have a bit of both however, favour one form of motivation more predominantly.

How to Motivate Yourself

There are many elements to motivation but in essence, each of us is primarily motivated to taking action in one of two ways. We are either motivated by the thought of moving TOWARD things or by moving AWAY FROM things.

"Toward" Motivation

Some people are motivated by the notion of moving toward things. This group gets excited by the thought of what they might achieve, or the pleasure that will be gained through the attainment of some task in the future. "Toward" people are usually goal orientated, entrepreneurial types who like "getting things done". They will find themselves waking from bed most easily by thoughts of the things they get to do in the day. They will be motivated to take a break from work by the thought of who they might be able to talk to, or what other things they might get done. Basically they move toward the things they want.

"Away From" Motivation

The other group of people are motivated by the notion of moving away from things that are painful or uncomfortable. This group takes action after the consequences of not taking action become too dire and they have to "avoid" some negative consequence. "Away from" thinkers are more aware of problems and they take action in a way that removes them from those problems as much as possible. "Away from" people will wake from bed in the morning at the thought of avoiding having their boss yell at them.

A good question to ask yourself is: "What are the positive and negative consequences of my actions?"

Let's take smoking as an example.

As discussed some people are motivated away from pain, for example: "If I don't give up smoking it could kill me," and some towards pleasure, instead thinking: "If I give up smoking I will feel fantastic and be able to go for runs."

It is very beneficial to know which category you fall into, so you can establish how to motivate yourself. You can find this out by identifying reasons as to why you do certain tasks.

What drives you to do certain tasks, as discussed earlier in the chapter, may hold the key and be the driving force strategy for you to accomplish future goals, and tasks.

Mastering Motivation

Being able to keep yourself continually motivated towards your goals on a daily basis is an invaluable skill that once mastered can go a long way to ensuring your success in any pursuit. While motivation is not the be all and end all of success, it's an aspect that very little can happen without. In actuality we are all motivated in many ways every day. Even if we are procrastinating and putting off taking action we are motivated, just toward a different end.

Understanding under which of these categories you fall into is essential to keeping continually motivated.

Tips For "Toward" Motivation

The most important thing for "toward" motivated individuals is to use the momentum that your energy for success will generate. You will get a lot of work done when you get on a roll of being continually excited about the tasks you are being set to perform. A toward person, your motivation will be increased the more frequently and more clearly you can look to the future at the things you want. You will feel a mental "salivation" by being able to clearly visualise the things you want and you will feel more compelled to pursue them. Take advantage of your toward motivation by focusing on what you want out of a situation when you feel your motivation waning. Concentrate on everything you will gain by completing a task and you will feel your energy immediately rise. Furthermore it will be helpful to keep the company of some "away from" motivated individuals who can bring you back down to earth and alert you to some of the potential problems involved in your lofty schemes.

Tips For "Away From" Motivation

If you are motivated by moving away from things the first thing you need to learn to do is "build the pain" quickly. Quite often you will find yourself not taking action until the pain becomes too great which means your progress will be slower. What you need to do is illustrate clearly the pain involved in not taking action and if necessary exaggerate it so that you won't wait too long to actually DO something. For example when your alarm goes off and you hit the snooze button you should get into the habit of illustrating clearly how much pain will be involved if you don't get up right now! Identify all the kinds of pain you will experience and in what quantities so that you will be "scared" in a way into taking action sooner rather than later. Sounds sadistic but that's how you people operate and there's nothing wrong with that! Also, you should develop a sturdy process for your review of problems that involves finding an end solution. You will find that analysing potential problems is only helpful up to a certain point after which you have to start looking at HOW you are going to avoid that problem i.e. thinking of a SOLUTION that will work for you. Finally as with "toward" motivated people, you will do well to keep the company of some of your counterparts who can give you a kick in the pants when you are taking too long to make decisions.

Which Style are You?

Exercise

Write a list of the activities and tasks you do during the week e.g. exercise, socialise, work.

And underneath the activities and tasks write down the reasons why you do them.

From the above descriptions and the above exercise you should already have some idea of which category you are in. Take a few minutes to monitor your thought patterns and notice whether you find yourself taking action when you are excited by things or when you are concerned by things. Also watch your language. Words like gain, achieve, accomplish, get, discover, learn, find etc. are toward words while ones like avoid, escape, save from, problem, won't have to, etc., are away from words.

Remember. Each style has its advantages and disadvantages the most important thing is realizing what motivates you personally and harnessing that force so that you can take continual loads of massive action. I trust this knowledge of motivation theory will allow you to take a big step forward in your ability to remain consistent and achieve your goals.

Now you have an understanding of your style of motivation, you can use this to create the leverage and underpin anything you want to achieve in your life.
And stay motivated.

Self-Talk

The power of words: Think of some of the most inspirational speeches you have heard; some of the greatest speakers and communicators of the last century, Winston Churchill, Martin Luther King. Thousands or even millions of people listening to every word said during powerful speeches. Or think of the closest people in your life that influenced you. It only takes one word, whether it is a negative or positive comment to have an influence on the course of your life.

I recall many years ago a colleague of mine who was a teacher told me a story of a young girl that was in his class. The young girl who was an excellent student, keen athlete and happy person, was at netball training one evening and being in her teens she was becoming conscious and aware of her figure. Her netball coach said your bum is looking bit bigger. This lead to a catalyst of events which would spiral the young girl into anorexia, it only took one word, and whilst it might not have been the only circumstances it may have been the trigger that pushed her over.

Words can have an impact on people, because the association to that word may have a much deeper implication or meaning. The same can be said in a positive way, a thank you, please, well done can go a long way.

Have you ever been into a shop to buy something, and the shopkeeper completely ignored your custom? Or you had done something well at work and nobody acknowledged you?

One of the most important people, if not the most important person you will ever communicate with is yourself.

At this point you are probably thinking, communicate with myself? Yes, we do communicate with ourselves and the impact our inner dialogue has on our life is immense, in this chapter I will explain how our inner dialogue works and provide you with exercises which can give your life a completely new perspective and meaning.

Often we are our own biggest critic, how we communicate to ourselves at times, our inner dialogue, can have a big influence on how we think and feel.

It has been established by psychologists and neuroscientists that we carry on an ongoing dialogue, or self-talk, of between 150 and 300 words a minute. This works out to a dialogue of between 45,000 and 51,000 words a day. Most of our self-talk is harmless dialogue that revolves around our daily activities like, "I need to stop at the shop to pick up some milk. I wonder what's on television tonight? What should we have for dinner tomorrow night?" The danger is when inner dialogue takes on a negative connotation such as, "I am too ugly to go out with a women like her," "I am useless, I always mess things up," or "I am not creative enough to learn art, I am tone deaf I could never learn to play an instrument, I haven't got the natural ability to play sport." The ongoing negative reinforcement created by habitual negative self-talk results in the creation of a limiting belief(s) that goes on to become a self-fulfilling prophecy.

Your parents, family, partners, teachers, coaches, friends have such an effect on you that their words can become buried in your brain and phrases echo around your head. Sometimes you hear your parents' comments in a situation you've experienced before only this time you're telling yourself the same thing! If you hear the same negative comments too often you may believe them and tell yourself what others think is true. Take a moment to think about your own inner self dialogue, and the impact it is having on your life, think of some of the words going through your mind.

It is estimated by research, that it's necessary for the ratio of positive to negative comments to be at least five to one for a relationship to be healthy and survive long-term. For these reasons, we're taught not to let others put us down. And equally as important not to put ourselves down.

Research also estimates the dialogue between parents to children in the western world is around eight negatives to one positive.

Our self-talk, or the words our inner dialogue uses when we think, can shape our lives, and influence our attitude and behaviour, and how we respond to certain situations, e.g. asking someone out on a date. Whether we stick to a healthily lifestyle plan, or take up something new, it can affect our happiness, can increase our stress levels, or limit our potential. It can influence our outlook on an experience and can almost become a self-fulfilling prophecy. If you keep telling yourself something, you may end up believing it.

Language can be influential

If you've been told by a colleague at work, that someone is completely useless, you will probably perceive that person as more incapable than if you've been told they "need assistance with certain tasks" or "need a bit of guidance".

Limited by our vocabulary

If you say I will never be good at this, I don't deserve it, I am stupid, "I can't do this," or "This is not for me." "I don't deserve it," you more than likely can't. This is because your subconscious mind tends to believe the thoughts it hears. You can limit your abilities by telling yourself you "can't", that "this is too hard," or that you "shouldn't even try".

I once had a client that had been on antidepressants for a few years. He was given a label, called a depressive. In his mind he adopted the belief he was a depressive. Although we had established there were times he wasn't depressed, like when he spent time with the children, and went out for a game of snooker with his mates. He went for walks with his wife which he loved and adored. We transferred his inner dialogue and after one session he came back to see me the following week and said he no longer needed tablets. His outlook on life and the person he thought he was completely changed. He rediscovered himself.

We did an exercise transforming his inner dialogue; the transformation of the inner dialogue shifted his focus and thought process into a more positive one. He has since gone on to enjoy a complete new quality of life, just by tweaking a few words.

Exercise

Just think about it for one moment. Take a few moments to think about and write down some of the things you say to yourself. Jot down a couple of phrases, words. As you write some of the things down, imagine the impact these words are having on your life.

How would you describe yourself in your relationships? How would you describe yourself as a person?

One of my clients once had a list of over 50 negative statements they were continuously saying to themselves over and over again in their mind. Whilst driving to work, they found themselves saying I hate this job, though I am too stupid to get a better job. Then every time they made a mistake at work they would call themselves a moron, a useless idiot, good-for-nothing. Even when he was on a date he would find himself saying she's out of my league, why would she go for a loser like me? And the list went on. I said to my client, who is the one person you love the most? He told me he loved his parents and family equally. I said would you say some of the things you say continuously to yourself to them? He said no, of course not. And I said why do you say it to yourself? Some of the things we find acceptable to say to ourselves, we wouldn't dream of saying to anyone else, as understandably, we wouldn't want to sabotage our relationships with the people who are important around us. Well the most important relationship you will ever have is with yourself.

Now let's look at some techniques you can implement to transform your inner dialogue.

Techniques to break negative states and strategies for positive self-talk:

→ Thought-Stopping: As you notice yourself saying something negative in your mind, you can stop your thought midstream by saying to yourself "Stop". Saying this aloud will be more powerful, and having to say it aloud will make you more aware of how many times you are stopping negative thoughts, and where.

→ Rubber Band Snap: Another therapeutic trick is to walk around with a rubber band around your wrist; as you notice negative self-talk, pull the band away from your skin and let it snap back. It'll hurt a little, and serve as a slightly negative consequence that will both make you more aware of your thoughts, and help to stop them! (Or, if you don't want to subject yourself to walking around with a rubber band on your wrist, you'll be even more careful to limit the negative thoughts!)

Turning a Negative into a Positive

1. Describe a situation in which you often tend to think/talk negatively to yourself.

2. Identify the negative statement you say to yourself.

3. Identify words or thoughts you can use to help you stop the negative thought.

4. List positive, beneficial statements you can use to replace your negative thoughts. These should be meaningful to you.

Positive Language

The main reason for giving a positive instruction is that the mind does not understand a negative instruction.

E.g. If I say to you don't think of the colour black, what do you think of? The very thing you were asked not to do! By using the principle of positive instruction; stating what you want rather than what you don't want, can have a powerful positive effect on the mind, but many people still tell themselves what they don't want, producing negative thoughts.

An example in football, a coach might say to his players don't lose the ball or when you shoot don't miss the target, might be the instruction, but would it not be better to instruct the player when he shoots to hit the target? Or keep possession. Phrases such as "don't foul", "don't lose the ball", and "don't lose the game" can all be replaced by more **Positive Instructions**

The same applies to different areas of our life. Like; have you ever told your children don't drop the glass, and bang they drop it, or told them don't be home late? And that's exactly what they process in their mind.

Communication Exercise Positive Self-Talk

List five negative instructions you say to yourself and replace them with a positive instruction.

For example you might make an error at work, and say to yourself you idiot you always get that wrong.

A more favourable instruction might be how can I learn from this and improve the situation? Remember focus on the outcome you want.

Negative Instruction

1. I am hapless I never learn.
2.
3.
4.
5.

Positive Instruction

1. I am an amazing person; I have learnt many tasks in the past and will do so in the future.

2.

3.

4.

5.

Watch your thoughts; they become words. Watch your words; they become actions. Watch your actions; they become habits. Watch your habits; they become character. Watch your character; it becomes your destiny.

Author Unknown

Communication Exercise Giving Instructions

List five negative instructions you give to your family, friends, colleagues and replace them with a positive instruction.

An example is you might say to someone, "Don't be late."

Replace that with, "I will see you at 7pm."

Another example in football is when the coach may say, "Don't lose the ball," to one of his players.

A more favourable instruction might be to, "keep possession". Focus on the outcome you want.

Negative Instruction

1.

2.

3.

4.

5.

Positive Instruction

1.

2.

3.

4.

5.

Transform your life by using the power of linguistics, the more you work at this the better an easier it becomes. This is a resourceful chapter you can revisit time and time again, however the impact of changing even one negative word to something more positive can completely change your mindset and outlook on life.

Chapter 8: Metaphorically Speaking

Metaphor is based on a Greek word meaning to carry something across or transfer.

"Float like a butterfly, sting like a bee."

Muhammad Ali

The power of a metaphor!

Do you remember story time back at school, or looking forward to having a bedtime story read by your parents? Some of the stories you heard when you were young, stories which would create an impact on your life, stories like Cinderella, the Ugly Duckling, no doubt you can think of many more. The impact some of these stories and metaphors had on your life allowed you to be able to draw from metaphors and stories to get a sense of perspective on your life. Such as the first time you had your heart broken, or experienced a level of rejection like not making the school cheerleading or football team; throughout our life it's these stories and metaphors that galvanise our resolve through our life's challenges.

Metaphors provide people with hope, and light, draw on our resources to be able to find a meaning from difficult and challenging situations. Metaphors provide us with multiple perspectives.

➜ One person's life can be the same old same old.

➜ And another person's life can be a bed of roses.

Which in turn can influence the way a person thinks or feels and approaches life.

Using metaphors we are able to step out of the problem and see it in a different context to help us find solutions and draw strength, draw upon all of our mind's resources. Metaphors are useful to be able to shift our mindset to a more creative resource, helping us to generate solutions, and reconnect with ourselves. The metaphors we already use can have a positive or negative impact on our lives; they can completely alter our perceptions on life and make an impact on how we feel and how we live our life.

A powerful example is I am sure the one we have all come across, same shit different day. I remember being a kid seeing people have it on little signposts on their car and even printed on tee shirts. Imagine waking up with that perspective on life, imagine how you would feel, think, what state of mind you would be in, probably not the best. I am sure we have come across and have possibly used many other negative metaphors for different parts of your life, for work, relationships.

Some examples of metaphors people use:

→ My life is like a roller coaster

→ Couldn't organise a piss-up in a brewery

→ Couldn't hit a barn door (metaphor used in football for someone who is struggling to score goals)

→ Have to kiss a few frogs before you find your prince

A metaphor can change your whole perception of a situation, a problem, your life, and in the process move you on to a new level, move you out of a problematic situation, put you in a more resourceful state of mind, make you happier, or give you hope.

(If you have ever watched the film *Forrest Gump*.) Forrest Gump says during a scene of the film: My momma always said, "Life is like a box of chocolates. You never know what you're going to get." Throughout the film, Forrest's attitude and outlook to life was one of anticipation, taking all of life's events in his stride.

A metaphor can be very influential in the way we live our lives, forming an attitude and becoming influential on our behaviour and outlook on life. When I was working with Bury Football Club, one of our players coming through would go on to achieve the most amazing success as a football player, having a meteoric rise to the top, from the depths of League Two to Champions League football.

I recall setting a physical training programme for the players where they would run tough 400 metre sprints, I don't think Colin particularly enjoyed this part of training, he would sometimes let me know his thoughts about doing the 400s, I used to say to Colin, you're a machine, you're built like a machine.

This was a metaphor which transformed the way he perceived the training.

I remember bumping into Colin when he was making his way up in the football league at a match, and one of the things he said was, I am a machine, which brought a smile to my face.

The following exercise is very powerful and can help you transform the way you feel about your life:

What are some of the metaphors you use in your life and think about the impact? If it has a negative impact change it to something more resourceful.

For example
- ➜ "We are all just a drop in the ocean."
- ➜ Change to something more profound, "By throwing a pebble into a river we can create a ripple."
- ➜ "At work I am just a number."
- ➜ To, "I am an important cog in a wheel."

Complete the exercise, write down the metaphors you are using to run your mind.

Take a few minutes to think about some of the metaphors you are using in your life.

Write the metaphors down.

Now think of the impact it is having on your life, the perception you gain from the metaphor.

From the list you completed the following exercise is to change anything negative to more positive.

Take a moment to think and notice how different you feel by creating a more resourceful metaphor.

Example

I am stuck in a dead-end job, can be changed to, my job is a stepping stone to better things.

My work...............

My relationships.........................

My life...

Using metaphors to create stories

This can be very therapeutic; having worked with many clients over a number of years this technique is a powerful and special technique to help people develop an inner resolve and greater perspective on many situations.

Some of the clients I work with have been through some of the most challenging experiences in life; they have suffered physical and mental abuse and get stuck in a negative place. Finding it difficult to move forward and make the most of their life, one of the techniques I use is to ask the client to come up with a metaphor for the situation they are going through in their life, it often has a powerful effect on their life.

I was working with a client once who had been on antidepressants for several years; they had been told that they were medically depressed by their GP. They told me how they felt, they had no hope, no motivation, found it difficult to get through life. They had given up all the things they enjoyed doing, cut themselves off from their friends and family, and were left in a dark place with no way out. Amongst many other things they said they had seen counsellors, doctors, psychologists; things never seemed to get better.

One of the techniques that helped them to move out of the situation they were in was that I had asked them to create a metaphor for the situation they were in and close the metaphor with a positive ending, the state of mind they would like to be in (so taking the present state of mind they were in and focusing on the desired state of mind). And having created the metaphor put it in a place they could see it daily.

Having done this, this person completely transformed their life, to the point they no longer needed medication, got back on their feet again, got a new job, revitalized their relationship, and took many social activities including dancing. They completely transformed their life, like many others, by altering their perspective. I am not advocating anyone on medication come off, though this is a perfect example of how sometimes we are too quick to label ourselves, or get labelled with something which isn't productive.

An example of a metaphor

For someone who is experiencing situations where things may be challenging, by persisting they can get through.

Consider a river; how it flows to the mighty seas, on its journey it meets many challenges and obstacles along the way, though never giving up hope, it keeps flowing.

The nature of the river is such no matter what gets in its way, hills, forests, fields; it manages to find a way round or through the obstacles until it succeeds in achieving its goal. Regardless of how difficult, challenging or impossible it may have seemed to begin with, the river keeps flowing until it meets the sea.

Create your own metaphor

Now, using the above metaphor as an example, do the following exercise with a situation in your life. Take the time to create a metaphor for a challenge you may be going through at the moment.

When creating your metaphor, take your time to relax and let your mind wander, let your subconscious mind take over and be creative.

Identify the situation or problem in your life.

Write down what's going on.

Who is involved?

How is it a problem?

How would you like things to evolve?

Key points in writing your metaphor:

→ In writing your metaphor decide on characters and settings that reflect the relationships of the people involved

→ Develop a plot that reflects the current problem

→ Develop the story reflecting the current problem into a story which has a positive ending

→ Making positive changes to the story build the metaphor

→ Populate the metaphor with characters (egg, superheroes, wizards, trees, birds, animals, people)

→ Populate the metaphor with what reflects the relationships of the significant people involved in developing the plot of the metaphor; include anything you may have already tried to change

→ Offer resolutions by developing the story so it moves towards a positive ending, be creative and draw from your subconscious mind

Having created your metaphor notice how differently you feel about the situation, your perspective and outlook.

Chapter 9: Believe in Yourself

"Whether you believe you can or you can't, you're absolutely right!"

Henry Ford

At one point it was believed the earth was flat and we could fall off.

In the first half of the 20th century the world believed that it was impossible to run a mile in under four minutes. When, on May 6th 1954, Roger Bannister ran a mile in 3.59 minutes, everyone was in awe. Then, a curious development took place. Within the following year many other runners ran the mile in under four minutes. It was as if a spell had been broken. To understand this phenomenon better, we have to take a closer look at our beliefs, and how they affect us. Beliefs guide our decisions and behaviour in all areas of life. They determine what we think is or is not possible. More often than not they prove to be self-fulfilling prophecies. Most of our beliefs are not fully our own, there is every chance they have been modelled from other people. Once a belief is formed, we work overtime to prove it right, even if the belief is something negative like, "I am worthless," or "I never get anything right." Many people are governed by their beliefs, even if they are harmful to others and ourselves.

Some of the negative beliefs I have come across from working with many clients over many years are: they will never find a partner, they don't deserve to be happy, they will never lose weight, they can't give up smoking, can't get motivated to exercise, and the list goes on.

To experience success in any area of your life, it is essential to have certain qualities. One of the most important qualities is belief. If you believe that you can achieve an outcome, your mind starts to recognise your positive qualities.

What is something you believed at some point you could not do or would be very difficult, though you managed to do it?

Example:

➜ Getting your driving licence at one point in your life might have seemed a world away

➜ Going to university

➜ Completing a 10km run

Write down a belief that you may have had about yourself that changed.

Write down certain beliefs you have in your life right now which are positive, e.g. good-looking, smart, intelligent.

Write down certain beliefs you may have in your life which you may or may not know where you picked up which are counterproductive e.g. never; going to be happy, find a good job, start a business, or find a partner.

Many limiting beliefs are characterised by terms such as:

- "Can't"
- "Need"
- "Have to"
- "Must"
- "Mustn't"
- "Should"
- "Shouldn't"

Technique to overcome negative beliefs

DO NOT challenge such limiting beliefs with the question "why?" or "why not?" Let's look at an example:

"I can't sustain a fulfilling relationship with a partner." I can't lose any weight, I must be happy, I shouldn't smoke, and I should exercise.

By asking the question "why not?" you are likely to elicit a list of reasons which only justify and reinforce the limiting belief rather than shifting it.

Ask What

The question focuses the brain in another direction. You are looking for practical suggestions within the person's control, solutions. Therefore it could be phrased more specifically. For example: What would have to be different for you to sustain a fulfilling relationship with a partner?

Lose weight, be happy, give up smoking, or exercise?

Creating leverage exercise releasing negative beliefs

Think of a negative belief you have about yourself at the moment or one that you wrote in the list earlier which isn't serving you.

Write down a negative belief you have which you want to release.

Now having written the belief down ask the following questions of the belief.

How is this belief ridiculous and absurd?

Was the person you learned this belief from worth modelling in this area?

What will it ultimately cost me if I don't let go of this belief?

What will it cost me emotionally if I don't let go of this belief?

What will it cost me in my relationships if I don't let go of this belief?

What will it cost me physically if I don't let go of this belief? What will it cost me financially if I don't let go of this belief? What will it cost family/loved ones if I don't let go of this belief?

Now having asked those questions how do you feel about that negative belief?

Is it worth keeping?

If not let it go, you don't have to believe anything about yourself you don't want to. You have a choice.

If you're still unsure and haven't found the leverage to break through the negative belief it might just mean, there is some work to be done in a certain area. E.g. you didn't just jump in a car and do a driving test. You took lessons and learnt. You have to work at it in certain areas and capabilities to build your belief to a level to go for it.

A useful exercise I use with my clients prior to setting goals and for releasing negative beliefs is a belief assessment sheet. This helps identify where you are in relation to working towards your goal. Certain beliefs can serve us. There is good reason at times for assessing our capabilities to achieve certain tasks. For example I was working with a client several years ago who wanted to run a marathon, though had never done any running before. Whilst they believed it was within their capabilities to run the marathon, he felt he needed to start with training and give himself a time frame he was comfortable with.

Take any outcome you're unsure of. Completing the following exercise will assist in building the capabilities or provide you with more leverage to go for your outcome.

Exercise

Belief Assessment Sheet

From a scale of one to ten with ten being the highest:

Do you believe your goal is achievable?

1 2 3 4 5 6 7 8 9 10

Do you believe you deserve your goal?

1 2 3 4 5 6 7 8 9 10

Do you believe your goal is appropriate and worthwhile?

1 2 3 4 5 6 7 8 9 10

Is your goal is desirable?

1 2 3 4 5 6 7 8 9 10

I know what I have to do to achieve my goal

1 2 3 4 5 6 7 8 9 10

I have the skills and capabilities to achieve my goal

1 2 3 4 5 6 7 8 9 10

Now identify any areas that you feel you need to develop and take action, with a sense of self-belief and certainty you will achieve your outcome in time. Just as you achieved other outcomes in your life.

Chapter 10: Getting into Shape

If you were given a five million pound racehorse, would you feed it crap, and not let it exercise, how are you investing in your most prized asset, yourself?

Without question your health is one of the most important aspects of feeling great. When you are feeling great it has a knock-on effect on other parts of your life, giving you a sense of well-being and confidence.

Exercise and activity stimulates your mind's endorphins (which are an essential part of feeling great). Have you ever done some exercise or played some sport and afterwards felt really great?

Exercise and activity are one of the best prescriptions for feeling better about yourself. Getting into shape has been the catalyst for many people to turn their life around, because if you feel better physically you're bound to feel better mentally.

Years ago through injury I had given up playing sport on a full-time basis, so I had gone from training from 4 to 5 hours per day, to next to nothing. I had completely let myself go, and whilst I was no longer training any more, I was eating the same amount, which was a fair bit. In no time I had gained a considerable amount of weight. I was carrying around 50 excess pounds; I was feeling sluggish, lacked energy, lost a considerable amount of self-esteem, and confidence. I had gone from being an excellent athlete with less than 5% body fat to carrying around 35% body fat, and whilst I don't advocate anyone to get down to 5% unless it's part of their sports regime and is controlled, having personally gone from 5% to 35% when around 12% to 17% is considered healthy for an adult male, 30% extra body fat from where I was before was a fair bit.

If you took 30% of 100 kilograms you would have 30 kilograms and that was the extra fat I was carrying, around 70 pounds of extra body fat.

Imaging carrying a 70 pound bag on your back all day. Almost like giving a piggyback to a small child all day. Imagine the impact it would have on your life, even during day-to-day tasks, shopping, going upstairs.

My goal was to once again start working in professional football as a fitness coach, I had to do something about not just my physique though, but how I felt about myself. I felt terrible and it was having a negative impact on my life, I felt like a slob. I knew I had to take action. And I did, I took up some sports I enjoyed, and changed my eating habits, within 6 months I was feeling much better, lighter, fitter, healthier. I didn't measure myself by the scale though, but by how I felt. In the process of losing that excess weight I felt much better, which was one of the best investments I made. Investing in my own well-being. Whilst I don't advocate overdoing it on exercise and eating rabbit food, being conscious of what you eat, and making time to exercise and be active goes a long way.

In this chapter I share some tips and techniques to help you get into great shape.

Remember if you're looking to lose weight

Losing weight isn't a mysterious process. In fact, weight loss doesn't even have to involve strange diets, special exercises or even the "magic" of pills or fitness gadgets. Want the secret to weight loss? Make small changes each and every day and you'll slowly (but surely) lose those extra pounds. The more food with high calories you eat and low nutritional values the more weight you gain. I am sure you're aware of that as you don't have to be a rocket scientist. It was something I was well aware of myself when I gained weight, after all I worked in the fitness industry for many years and as an athlete. I knew enough about nutrition to understand by continuing to eat the volume and type of food I was eating I was going to keep on gaining weight. However what many people seem to think is by doing some exercise it will burn off all the calories they have consumed.

Exercise has many benefits other than burning calories; it can help lower heart rate, lower blood pressure, make you feel better, stimulate the mind, and contribute towards minimising the risk of illness. Though in regards to losing weight exercise can contribute to losing weight, though the calorie expenditure during exercise is minimal, so what we eat is the key to losing weight. To put it into context a one hour run from your normal adult will burn around 300 calories.

Some chocolate bars have double the calories an hour run has.

To lose one pound, you must burn approximately 3,500 calories **over and above what you already burn doing daily activities**. In other words a sensible nutritional plan with exercise and activity are the ingredients to losing weight and staying in shape. The irony is when people join a gym they sometimes gain more weight; because they feel they are burning the weight off. I have seen many people, go do a session in the gym, and then an hour later they're in the bar having a pint.

Nutrition and calories

McDonald's double cheeseburger contains around 460 calories.

To burn off the calories in just that *one* burger, the average 150-pound person would have to do moderate intensity aerobics for an hour!

Add on a shake and an order of fries and you might as well cancel any plans you had for the half a day you'll need to spend at the gym to undo that one meal!

Good nutrition is very important for fat loss, and focusing on health and health promoting foods is far more productive than focusing on fat loss and denial of favourite foods.

I am sure reading this you might be thinking I find the gym boring or I don't have time to go to the gym. I guess there's nothing more patronising then some young 20-year-old gym instructor telling you to make time, especially if you're very busy or logistically getting to the gym for you on a regular basis is difficult.

Exercise does not have to involve going to the gym, albeit some people enjoy going to the gym, there are many other ways to get in shape, which burn equally as many calories and have equally as many health benefits, like organising a game of five-a-side football with your mates. Or going for a country walk with your partner, here's a list of other things you can do too:

Make Exercise Fun

1 Swimming
2 Classes
3 Sports: such as badminton, tennis, squash, anything you enjoy
4 Gym circuit training
5 Dancing
6 Horse riding
7 Rock climbing
8 Table tennis

The list is not exhaustive, identify activities you enjoy doing and integrate them into an activity plan. Doing the activities you enjoy will help you to stay motivated and contribute towards a healthier lifestyle.

Simple nutritional changes

You can start losing weight **right now** by making a few simple changes. If you can burn around an extra 500 calories each day, you could lose around a pound a week. Try these ideas:

Instead of:	Do this:	Calories:
Having an afternoon Coke	Drink a glass of water	Saved - 97
Eating a bacon sandwich for breakfast	Eat some fruit and cereal	Saved - 185
Using your break to catch up on work or eat a snack	Go for a walk	Burned - 100

Waking up 5 minutes early	Get up 10 minutes early to do some exercises. e.g. abdominal crunches	Burned - 100
Watching television after work	Do 10 minutes of yoga	Burned - 50

Complete the following goal setting process to get you well on the way to losing weight and staying in shape:

Have a goal: e.g. sign up for a 5km fun run.

1. State your goal in the positive.

Think about what you want rather than what you don't want. If you still come up with something negative ask yourself, "What do I want instead?" In the context of weight loss what do you want?

2. State it in simple terms.

If a five-year-old wouldn't understand it, it may be too complex – unlike some goal setting techniques your goal needs to be brief, simple and specific. E.g. how many pounds do you want to lose and when, what dress size would you like to fit in to, what size jeans?

3. State it in the present tense.

Make it as if it is happening now. I have, I am, I'm doing... what are you doing right now?

4. Is it achievable and realistic?

Has someone else already achieved this or might they achieve this? Is it realistic for you? If one person can achieve something then so can you.

5. Set a time and make it an exciting outcome.

There is some debate about setting a date and some people feel uncomfortable about this. If it is a small goal then do it. If it is a really big goal then I advise that you leave the time for the moment until it starts to look like things are moving.

6. Finally how will you achieve your goal?

For example:

By going to the gym twice a week, going for a walk twice per week, changing certain things you eat, doing things in a manageable way to suit your lifestyle, choose exercises and activities you enjoy. Remember not to overestimate what you can achieve in a week and underestimate what can be achieved in six months.

Remember losing weight and staying in shape is a lifestyle change. There are many diets and fads on the market which people lose a lot of weight in a short amount of time, only to put it back on and to risk their health. One of the things I tell my clients is you didn't put the weight on overnight, or in two weeks, the weight you put on was through a gradual process of neglect, creeping up on you. To expect to lose all the weight you may have accumulated in a few years, in just two weeks, probably isn't feasible.

By making a few changes to what you eat, doing some activity and exercise you enjoy, and integrating into a lifestyle change you are building an effective platform to staying in shape and never looking back.

Chapter 11: See Things from a Different Point of View

"Do not judge your neighbour until you walk two moons in his moccasins."

Cheyenne Proverb

Have you ever thought a certain way about a situation, only to see it completely differently at another time in your life? How about certain situations in our life, relationships with our friends, family, work colleagues, your partner?

Have you ever been hurt by someone? Feel let down, had a disagreement with someone close to you and carried those emotions for a long period of time? Or felt you were a victim of someone's actions and found it difficult to move forward with your life? Or you wanted a member of your family to live their life in a certain way, have your expectations for someone else?

I once did this exercise, which we'll go through later in the chapter, with someone who hadn't spoken to another member of their family for over 50 years. They picked up the phone a day after doing this exercise and decided to phone their brother and look to repair the damage of an argument they had 50 years earlier. Soon after they reunited, and decided to become a part of each other's life. Sometimes we can see things in a blinkered way, without considering another person's thoughts and feelings. It is easy to pass judgment on how someone else may handle a situation, though what is more of a challenge and may provide us with a valuable insight is seeing it from another point of view.

The techniques in this chapter are very powerful when used in our personal life to resolve conflict, in business to alter our perception, in sport to gain a stronger understanding of colleagues, opposition, critics, and fans. And even times where you are the victim, by seeing things from a different perception we can move forward in a positive way in our life.

I once worked with a lady who had been in an abusive relationship for many years. Her husband was very abusive for many years physically and mentally.

Growing up she had abusive parents, she said she felt low, wasn't sure if she could move forward with her life. She had come out of her marriage after 40 years, and felt emotionally tied to the abuse she had suffered over many years.

Whilst it was hard for her to do, we looked at things from the point of view of her parents and her husband, by doing the exercise perceptual positions, her response was that she finally felt free and alive again. She was able to let go of the emotions and negative feeling. She felt her parents only did what they knew, they didn't know any better, their parenting was the best they could do in a difficult time for them. She realised her husband all along was the one with the issues of insecurity which he manifested into abuse towards her. That was it, she was no longer going let what happened in her past dictate her future. It was time to let go, and do some living, and living she did. My client took their life to a new level even enrolling at college to study a course, amongst many other positive changes. They let go of feelings of resentment and pain, claiming her life back, as feeling the way she did and behaving the way she was, was affecting only one person and that was her.

Whilst I don't condone people who harm and hurt other people, I believe they also don't have the right to continue to affect people emotionally through the actions they did. And as an individual you can, by understanding their perception, let go of any negative feelings and claim your life back. Perceptual positions are a powerful exercise and later in the chapter I have specific techniques for personal life, business and sport.

Different perceptions

It was around about the time of the 9/11 attacks on the World Trade Center in New York. I was working on a coaching programme with different clients who had flown over to Manchester, UK, to work with me from all over the world. In particular I had a client of mine who lived in Qatar whose family was from Palestine originally, though they had left Palestine to move away to Qatar from the unrest that had been going on from Israeli bombing. On the other hand I had a client over from the USA and another who was Jewish who lived in the UK, who had said they left Israel to move away from the unrest which was caused by attacks.

Throughout the first day of the programme I could feel a level of tension and unease with what had happened in New York, with the World Trade Center terrorist attacks. Sensing the tension I asked them to tell me a little bit about how they felt individually. They told me about all the suffering they had gone through as result of what was happening politically. On one hand my client from Qatar told me how his family had to leave Palestine due to Israeli bombing, and how he had lost family and friends through bombing over the years. He told me how up until the 1940s it used to be

Palestinian homeland and explained Palestine had to make way for divisions of land to accommodate the Jewish people.

On the other hand my client who was Jewish spoke of how she had lost family and friends from Palestine attacks in Israel. Whilst I wasn't in a position to express my thoughts on the situation, I didn't understand politically the intricacies of the situation, it wasn't my place to pass any judgment. I found both my clients to be good people with many good qualities and it was a pleasure working with them.

And I guess with the programme I was running, in the broad scheme of things with what was going on in the world, I felt I had to give them the opportunity to defer to another time if they wanted to. Both my clients wanted to carry on with the training programme, as they had made their commitment.

However I sensed a bit of unease. With that in mind, I commended them for making the commitment to stay on, and suggested we did the following technique, perceptual positions, which I believed would help them to reach a level of understanding for each other, hence helping them to get the most out of the training programme which was running over the next six weeks.

Having done perceptual positions on both clients, they both could see things from each other's point of view. Whilst that didn't solve any of the world's problems it helped two people put any differences to one side for six weeks and a lifetime after that. Perceptual positions is a powerful exercise which requires skill and strength and character to be able to see things from a different point of view.

What are Perceptual Positions?

The perceptual positions exercise is taken from Neurolinguistic Programming (NLP). Its goal is to show you, in a structured way, how to see other people's points of view. It's a straightforward exercise that you can do in just a few minutes.

Here's an example of how you would benefit from a perceptual positions exercise. Imagine you have been disappointed with your children. You asked them to tidy their room and they haven't managed to do it. When you go up to check whether they have tidied the room you realise they have barely made a start. You become angry, and begin to think they were lazy, couldn't be bothered, they disrespected you by not doing it, they never listen and the list goes on. On the other hand the reason the children didn't tidy their room, is because they stayed up late the last two nights trying to finish an assignment they were finding difficult. They were having a hard time at school and wanted to talk to you, though you were too tired as you came in from work just before they went to bed, and as soon as you got in you switched on the television and slumped on the sofa.

Situations like this can be frustrating. However, like most things in life, there are usually two sides to the story. A technique like perceptual positions can help you understand another person's perspective and perception; so that you can both communicate with each other more constructively, and work out a resolution.

The perceptual positions exercise can work on a variety of different areas of our lives helping us to resolve conflict, find a solution and think of a way to go forward.

The Perceptual Positions Exercise

The perceptual positions exercise allows you to look at a situation from three different viewpoints: your own, the other person's, and that of an objective outsider. Follow these steps to take yourself through the technique.

Step 1: Identify the situation

Start by identifying a specific situation for which you want to build a positive relationship. We'll continue to use the example of the parent and child.

Step 2: Set up your space

Using this technique, you move to an entirely different place in the room every time you "change positions" (become someone else). This doesn't have to be a major change – for example, you could simply switch chairs in your living room or kitchen. However, it's important to set up three separate locations before you begin.

The reason why it's useful to change spaces is because this allows you to take a break from each viewpoint you'll be experiencing. Think of it like wiping the slate clean and readying yourself to write something new. In NLP we call this "breaking state", and physically changing positions for each viewpoint is important to the success of this exercise. Make sure you know which space you'll use for each viewpoint; for example, when you're being yourself. When you take your child's position, you'll sit in a different chair. And when you're the objective outsider, you'll sit in the chair across the room.

Step 3: Get to know each position (person)

Before you start dealing with a specific issue, familiarise yourself with the different positions you'll experience.

This is similar to trying on new clothes. Simply imagine what it's like to be "inside" each different person. Think of it as role playing. Don't focus on your specific situation yet.

It's important to imagine as much detail as possible. For instance, if you're taking your child's position, think about his/her hand gestures, his/her mannerisms, and her viewpoints. Hear their voice as they talk, and try to imagine how they feel in different situations. Really put yourself into the role, much like an actor would. For just a minute or two, try to "become" the other person.

In perceptual positions, there are three commonly used positions. Practice each position for just a minute:

➔ First position   This is you

➔ Second position   This is the other person
                             involved in the situation (in
                             this case, your child or person
                             you have conflict with)

➔ Third position   This is an objective outsider,
                             someone you respect or

admire though has no
connection with or
involvement in the situation

Every time you switch positions, take a quick break, and do something entirely different to free your mind of that role.

You could drink some water or read a paragraph from a book. This will help your mind "leave" one role so you can easily change to the next.

Step 4: Explore each position

Now you're ready to start imagining your specific situation.

First position

Go to your first point, the physical space you chose for your first position (e.g. chair in the living room). Close your eyes, and review the specific situation in your mind. Picture it exactly as it happened, seeing it through your own eyes. Remember exactly what each person said, and how you felt.

The more specific you are, the better the exercise will work.

Second position

After you replay the situation clearly from your viewpoint, take a break. Get up and do something else for 15 seconds. Then, move to your second position's point (in our example another chair in the living room).

Imagine the situation from the other person's point of view. Imagine stepping into your children's bodies and becoming them, and look at yourself through their eyes. Replay again what you both said – but this time, try to imagine their perspective. What is the understanding of the situation? How do they see you and your actions?

Third position

Once you've completely replayed the situation, take another quick break. Then step into the position of the objective outsider, someone who you respect or admire, who is watching like a fly on the wall, moving to the third point (in our example, the chair across the room).

For this last position, it's helpful to picture yourself looking down on the scene from above, or looking through a window into the room. You could also imagine yourself as a counsellor, listening objectively to both sides of the story.

Ask yourself these questions: How are these two people acting? Are they being fair to each other? Are they listening to what each other has to say? Is the present behaviour resolving anything? Is one being dominant, while the other is submissive? What advice would you give these two people to help them work out their differences?

Step 5: Analyse what you've learned

Take a few minutes to write down what you learned from the exercise. What did you learn about yourself? What did you learn about the other person? How do you want to move forward from here?

Key Points

The perceptual positions technique allows you to see things from someone else's perspective by replaying a scene from the viewpoints of yourself, the other person, and an objective outsider. You may get a clearer picture of what actually happened – and how the other person sees the situation. This technique may take some practice, but the more you do it, the easier it will become.

Perceptual positions exercise for business

Another area where I use perceptual positions is in business, not only to resolve conflict though, but to see things from your customer's point of view.

I once worked with directors of a major company who had been experiencing difficulty, business was slowing down; the relationship between staff, management and technicians, was breaking down. Things were going only one way, towards rock-bottom.

I had asked the directors to have management work as technicians for one day and have a couple of technicians to spend a day in management. Reluctantly at first, but due to the situation the company was in they decided to give the exercise a go, doing a role reversal between the two parties who were not happy with each other; some management staff and some technicians.

What both parties realised were the challenges they both faced; technicians realised the pressure management were under in an industry which was highly competitive. Management realised some technicians didn't have the tools to do certain jobs, due to financial cutbacks, and some technicians were feeling down due to not being paid on time.

This process resulted in an action plan to resolve issues; with the insight and understanding the company could now take action on key issues to resolve conflict, improve relationships amongst staff and create a more positive environment. Had they not have seen things from each other's point of view, nothing may have been done, to the detriment of the company. Yet seeing things from each other's position, a positive solution was secured.

Client's point of view

I also use the technique to assist people develop their business, as the most important people in any business are the clients.

Too often it's easy to get wrapped up in our day-to-day goings on without ever stopping to think of what anyone else thinks. Sometimes we may think we are right and can blinker ourselves from seeing the big picture and the danger is if we don't open our mind we won't fulfil our potential.

I was working with someone who had set up a new business and did all the market research preparation necessary, had put together a business plan, and an action plan, though things were still not working out.

We did the following perceptions technique and as a result I received a call from them a few weeks later to let me know they were securing several orders. Something they managed to do just by tweaking a few things, by seeing things from the point of view of their customers.

The ability to see things from the point of view of another, e.g. your existing clients, customers and future potential customers, is crucial to success.

<u>Why use this?</u>

→ Enables you to view your business through your customer's eyes.

→ How beneficial do they see your products or services being for them?

→ Helps you retain existing business and attract more business.

→ What they the customer are looking for in your product or service? How your product or service makes them feel.

→ How do they rate your product or service in comparison to your competition? Why would they choose to spend money with your company rather than with your competition?

→ Improves your understanding of your clients, customers, potential customers and helps you become more aware of your customers reasons to buy.

→ Helps you appreciate the influence of your verbal and non-verbal behaviour on others, your sales process and the influence of their behaviour on you.

→ Understanding and appreciating others' points of view is the cornerstone for building a winning team.

Perceptual Positions Technique for Generating Business:

First Position

This is your own perceptual position as you, yourself, and your role within your business or the company you work for. In NLP, we would call this a fully associated position. That is, you are fully in it and living it as if it is happening right now.

Second Position

This is the perceptual position of an "other". It's the walking, seeing, hearing, feeling, thinking, etc., in another person's shoes.

For example, your existing client, customer, potential customer, competitor.

Step into your customer's shoes and mind and look at your business from their point of view, by closing your eyes, relaxing and imagine being your customer/client as they see you/your product.

Write down any key points you gain from the different perspective.

Third Position

Think of someone who you admire or respect, who is looking at your business and customers from a third position. The third position is in the eyes of an observer involved in gathering information and noticing what is happening between your customers and your business. Step into their shoes and mind and notice what is happening, close your eyes relax and see the interaction between your clients and customers, and your business detached from a different perspective.

Write down key points from the different perspective.

What have you learnt? How do your customers currently view your business? How can you use the information learnt to better your business? E.g. improve customer service, make your product cheaper/dearer. Bring in new measures to improve the image of business, product.

Perceptual positions exercise for sports coaches and athletes

Another area where I use perceptual positions is when I am working with coaches and athletes. I remember we were playing a football match against a team which was in a higher league than us, and at half-time the players had given it their all and knew they had been through a game.

The manager picked up on this and told the players however you feel, imagine the other team, what they must be thinking. I could see a boost in the players' faces just by associating to how the other team may have been feeling.

Knowing they were pushing a team in a higher league to the limit.

Or sometimes as a coach it is easy to get frustrated with the players/athletes where things aren't going as well as we would like.

This is also a worthwhile exercise with sports participants and fans, fans appreciate the effort players put in, and players appreciate the extent fans go to supporting their teams.

It is also a worthwhile exercise to see things from a referee's point of view which can be the most difficult role in the game. That frustration does not resolve anything. It is worth seeing things from a different point of view.

"Think of a situation or an incident through the eyes and ears of others; and you will soon find better ways of managing similar occurrences. The steps are easy."

Have you ever been in a tense situation in a game, or a player has made a mistake in a game, have you been in a difficult situation in a game and wondered how you could have done it better? This tip will help you to look at an incident from different viewpoints. This should help you to find ways of managing similar future situations in a much better way. Consider a single difficult situation that you have been in recently, by thinking about it from three different perspectives:

1. Yourself (the coach).

2. The player.

3. An observer (perhaps an assessor, manager or a spectator).

When you explore perceptual positions, you will start to develop an ability to experience interaction in a new way. You will learn to see and to hear, and to feel the relationship through the eyes and the ears and the emotions of the player. You also develop the ability to explore the relationship through the eyes and ears of a neutral observer (a fly on the wall, a hidden video camera, a spectator, etc.). When you add these new dimensions to your current self-assessment, you will learn new ways of behaving that will enrich and enhance each and every relationship you have with players. You do this by putting yourself in their shoes, and by asking yourself how you would have felt in the same behavioural situation.

Technique for sports coaches:

Step 1 of 6:

As you think about a difficult situation or a specific situation in a game or whilst coaching, you begin to remember other times when things did not go quite as well as you would have liked them to. As you mull this over in your mind, you start remembering the interaction (history) in greater detail.

Step 2 of 6: Through Your Own Eyes:

First, you see the experience through your own eyes, becoming aware of what trouble the player gave you. You hear the experience through your own ears, listening to what the player is saying, what you are saying out loud, and what you were thinking to yourself at the time. You experience what it is like to be with this player. What you feel about the player, and also about your behaviour during the interaction. Then you freeze the interaction and notice what you have learnt about yourself. It is here, that you can perceive better ways of dealing with the situation, such as; controlling (or hiding) your emotions; better positioning; ways to be stronger or more polite, and making your instructions clearer for the listener, etc.

Step 3 of 6: Through the Player's Eyes:

See the experience through the player's eyes, becoming aware of what you look like from his perspective. You hear the experience through the player's ears, listening to what you are saying. You feel what it is like to be the player, what you feel about yourself from here. Then you freeze the interaction and notice what you have learned about yourself and the player. It is here, that you can imagine what the player thought about you, as you were dealing with him. Would it have worked better if you had been calmer; or had used different words; or perhaps used more authority; or by being more friendly and polite, etc.? Did you really need to embarrass him? These are the questions seen from the player's perspective. Next time this incident happens, you should now be able to temper your approach to eliminate the things that did not originally work.

Step 4 of 6: Through the Eyes of an Observer:

See the experience through the eyes of an observer who might be neutral. You listen to the coach and the player talking to one another. You become aware of how they have interacted together previously in the game and notice any patterns and repetitions. Then you freeze the interaction and perceive what you have learned about yourself (the coach) and the player. Was there a clash of two strong characters? Who was in charge of the situation? Was the situation resolved in a satisfactory way? How was the situation managed? Etc.

Step 5 of 6: Using the new Perceptions to Improve

What have you learnt?

What could you do to resolve any issues or improve your ability to handle different situations which may arise?

One of life's challenges is to be able to have the strength to see things from a different point of view, sometimes it is not easy to see things from a different point of view as it might highlight flaws we may have ourselves. As much as we like to believe we are always right, or sometimes we may be hurt or upset and feel victimized by someone's actions, we may feel seeing a situation from someone else's point of view is irrelevant. Or we may feel that it's not resourceful or we don't want to go there.

The art of seeing things from a different point of view is an opportunity for us to take action, release any negative emotions, take a level of responsibility to move things forward and affect things in a positive way.

Chapter 12: Modelling Excellence

The Difference that makes the Difference

One of the most efficient ways to help you achieve your goals or what you want out of life is to find someone who has achieved what you're aiming for and learn what they did. This process will save you a lot of time and provide invaluable insights.

One of the NLP presuppositions is: possible for you, possible for me, just a matter of how.

We all have a brain which has exceptional capabilities; if one person has the capability of doing something then so can someone else.

If you were going to run a marathon for the first time would you ask for tips and advice from someone who has done one before or someone who hasn't?

How many young bands have been inspired by the Beatles?

- ➜ Entertainers by Madonna
- ➜ Football players by Pelé
- ➜ Young boxers by Muhammad Ali
- ➜ Writers by Steven King
- ➜ Basketball players by Michael Jordan

How does Cristiano Ronaldo become one of the best footballers in the world?

Michael Phelps become one of the greatest swimmers of all time?

Sir Richard Branson one of the world's most successful entrepreneurs?

Over many years of studying people one question I like to ask successful people is who and what inspired you?

I have always enjoyed for many years, even as a child, listening to interviews on radio, watching interviews on TV, reading journals, books and biographies to see who had been the inspiration behind people's success.

Role models are people who influence our lives; we are in essence a product of the people we decide to model. Sometimes it can have a positive effect on our life and sometimes a negative effect.

Particularly in our childhood, role models have a big impact on our lives. I was at a coaching awards ceremony once where I was nominated for a coaching award and the guest speaker was an Olympic swimming medallist and in his speech, he talked about how at an early age, he saw an Olympic athlete dressed in their full Olympic uniform and it inspired him to want to do the same. It was almost as if that moment was a spark of inspiration, which would transform his life.

Time for reflection

Complete the following exercise:

Everyone has been influenced by other people in their life. If you are a parent, have you said the same things to your children, your parents said to you?

Think about it for a few seconds, whose behaviour have you modelled, who have been the people you have modelled?

It could be a parent, a friend, a teacher, or a sports hero.

Exercise

1. Who were the people in your life that had the most impact?

2. How have they influenced you?

3. What are some of the things that serve you from adopting their behaviour and some things that don't?

Whilst we are influenced by different people in different areas of our life, for example our capabilities to do tasks, our value base, our beliefs about ourselves and who we become, some of what we have modelled has a positive impact on our life and serves us well. However in other parts of our lives some of the things we modelled might not be productive.

For example:

→ We may think we not cut out for business

→ Not cut out for relationships

→ Not cut out to play sport, sing, or write a book

Some of the things we have modelled may be negative beliefs, though we may not have known any better.

Life sometimes is about timing − if we meet the right person under the right circumstances then it opens up many possibilities. However we don't need to leave things to chance, there are plenty of people out there we can learn from if we have something we would like to achieve, skills and capabilities we would like to learn, resources we would like to acquire.

Learning from people who have mastered and are getting results in an aspect or area of their life we wish to get similar results, gives us an amazing and powerful insight. It also makes us realise we are all human, we all make mistakes and nobody is perfect. If one person can get into their best shape ever so can someone else, if one person can write a book, write a song, run a marathon, run a successful business, or be happy and confident then so can someone else.

"We all have the same neurology, so if one person can do something, it is possible to model it and transfer it to ourselves and or teach it to others."

Modelling involves identifying people – or teams and organisations – that are excellent, and eliciting what precisely they do (i.e. their behaviours) and, probably even more importantly "how they do it" when they are "being excellent".

We know that excellent behaviour comes from a level of unconscious competence, what are often referred to as "habits" – i.e. when we are "being excellent" we are not thinking about what we are doing, we simply do it!

For example, have you ever delivered a presentation which went amazingly well, made a speech, did well in a sports event, and you were in the zone. You didn't have to think about what you did, you just did it – that is operating out of the unconscious where we barely even notice time, everything flows.

In NLP it is presupposed that, "If one person can do something then anyone can learn to do it". Talent is learned and not inherited! What we take to be natural ability is actually a set of values, beliefs and unconscious behaviours that have been learned, perhaps by chance, and then reinforced by subsequent experience.

In other words much of behaviour and skills and capabilities are learnt. At one time tying your shoelaces was new, you learnt it and it became a skill, you tie your shoelaces now without thinking. Driving a car at one time was something new, through being taught over time you learnt how to do it and it became a skill you can do without thinking. At one time you may have been told to speak only when you are told to and that became behaviour or belief, or you were told to ask and you will receive that also became a belief and behaviour, all of which are learnt.

So if one has the desire they can become all they wish to be.

Exercise

Write all the things you are capable of e.g. playing an instrument, a sport, performing a task, or a skill, behaviour such as confidence, performing a task or belief about yourself.

When did you learn the capability? And how did you learn the capability?

Learn the modelling process so you can achieve excellence, in business, sport and your personal life.

In outline, the NLP modelling process is to identify an expert, and to elicit the underlying values and beliefs that relate to the context. Then we map the "strategies" that they use, the actual steps in thinking and acting that they perform. If you're looking to start a new business, find someone who is successful in business, if you're looking to be more confident find someone who is confident, if you're looking to improve public speaking find someone who is excellent at public speaking, if you're looking to write a book find someone who has written good books, if you're looking to take your company to a higher level find a company which is at a higher level, the list goes on depending on what you would like to learn or accomplish, if they learnt it so can you.

In a physical skill, such as serving a tennis ball, performing a football skill, shooting a basketball, the mental state is crucial to making the muscles act together in the desired sequence. In an interpersonal skill, such as influencing, the mental state will also be reflected in external behaviour. This time though it is language, tonality, pace, gestures, posture, breathing, facial expression etc. to which others unconsciously respond.

Modelling excellence has been at the heart of my work, from modelling successful businesses to creative writers, people who were getting results in different aspects of their life.

I even modelled people and organisations which were not successful and compared them to successful strategies and noticed the difference which, on many occasions, was only minimal. Millimetres separated the top and mediocre and by employing this strategy someone achieving average results could improve beyond belief.

When I first starting working with Bury Football Club's youth team, my aim was to put together a programme to help develop players to their potential. My search began to find a template or templates we could learn from.

My first port of call was Manchester United Football Club as they had been producing world-class players such as Ryan Giggs, Paul Scholes, David Beckham to name a few. Manchester United being one of the biggest clubs at the time, had resources we could only dream of, however I believed it was possible to learn what they were doing in training and use some of their methods and techniques. The other teams and organisations I would look at to name are few were the Australian Institute of Sport, Ajax FC, and Crewe Football Club which was possibly nearer to the size and infrastructure of our club.

There was a huge variation between the teams and organisations I modelled because we didn't have the resources and infrastructure of the bigger clubs, and it was in my opinion that many of the smaller clubs didn't have the psychological mindset. Through the modelling I elicited some key strategies.

The first thing I told my players was I am introducing fitness tests. I was fortunate to obtain the fitness test results of a top Premiership team at the time and I set the players a goal of achieving the same levels of fitness.

I.e. if a top Premiership player can run 3,500metres in 12 minutes and less than 3 seconds for a 20metre sprint, that is your target as a player. And because football is a physical sport, statistically you only touch the ball for around 3 minutes in a 90 minute game, the value of being in top shape is immense, which would break a massive belief barrier. The psychological boost for a footballer to know physically they are as fit to participate in football as the leading players is a massive boost, particularly as the physical component of the game is of such an importance. However the physical ability is not the be all and end all, key components are technique, tactics, belief, confidence and other psychological resources which can all be modelled.

So the template of excellence was created by a combination of a few different clubs: what levels they were physically, what they were doing technically and tactically, what were they eating. And most importantly what was going through the mind of these players at the highest level.

What did they believe about themselves, their teammates? How did they walk, talk, what did they think and feel?

What were their beliefs and values, about themselves and football? My aim was to get into the mind of the best footballers and transfer it to my players, bearing in mind that the average percentage of players that graduate from youth team football to play professionally is around 10%. I wanted to smash that and some.

In the beginning just introducing fitness tests and using a measurable target to show the players they were on a par physically with some of the best players in the country was enough to build massive belief and confidence. However that was only the start, we had broken one barrier, we were going to break even more.

The players we went on to produce were people like, Colin Kazim Richards, Nicky Adams, David Worrall and the list goes on, as a result of raising the bar and replicating excellence, on a tight budget and with scarce resources.

This same principle I have used with other sporting infrastructures, athletes, business people, sales representatives, people looking to develop positive character traits such as confidence, motivation, happiness, to assist in improving the quality of their life, get in good shape, and take a positive step forward and punch above their weight.

Behavioural modelling is the study of how people get results – whether these results are coded as "successful" or "unsuccessful"...

Behavioural Modelling is the study of what accounts for the results that people achieve. In other words, what are the thoughts, behaviours, skills, beliefs, values, and other attitudinal qualities that they use to do what they do? Behavioural Modelling can be used to discover the key components of thinking, feeling and behaving that someone at the top of their field uses.

The key is when you recognise someone as being successful in what they do, how do you define what it is that makes them such a good performer?

The modelling process is one I have used with businesses, sports teams, and individuals looking to excel in a specific area. It is not everyone's aspiration to become a top-class athlete or high-flying business person. For some people it might be writing a book, losing a few pounds, giving up smoking, taking part in a fun run.

We can all learn from people who are achieving what it is we are aiming to achieve.

How you may ask, do I perform the technique?

First let's look at some key points.

The Structure of Experience

All of what we experience in life is comprised of various elements: behaviour, emotions, patterns of thinking, and the beliefs or assumptions on which those patterns are based. Differences in experiences are a direct result of differences in how these elements are structured. That is, your behaviours, what you are feeling, what you are thinking, what you believe, and how all of these elements interact with one another, combine to give rise to your experience at a moment in time. That array of content and relationships constitutes the structure of the experience.

It is within these structures that we find the differences that distinguish someone who is adept at an ability from someone who is not. In modelling, we are "mapping" out the underlying structure of experience that makes it possible for someone who is excellent in their field to manifest his/her particular ability. If we – or anyone – structure our experience to match that of the person who is excellent in their field, that structure will enable us to manifest (to a great extent) that same ability.

Modelling, then, is the process of creating useful "maps" (descriptions of the structure of experience) of human abilities.

→ Such maps are useful because they allow us to understand the experiential structure that makes it possible for a person to manifest a particular ability.

→ Such maps are useful because they can make it possible for anyone to have that experience or ability by making that map their own.

Having found a positive role model you need to work out what they are doing differently. You need to look at what they do. That is the physical side of things such as posture, timekeeping and body language.

For example:

When they are delivering a presentation

→   Communicating effectively
→   Performing a sports technique or skill
→   Delivering a sales speech

Think of someone who has exceptional capabilities and watch their physiology whilst they perform the task carefully. Though studying just the physical element isn't enough, we need to also find out what is going through their mind, to support their ability.

I remember when the successful football manager Jose Mourinho first started working in the UK Premiership, and during a press conference he called himself the special one. Whilst many people were taken by surprise by the comment, my own thoughts were this is a belief he has, which has obviously had a positive impact in his career as a football manager. There were many other coaches I am sure had as much knowledge as Jose Mourinho, after all he wasn't recognised for his playing ability, he never played football at a level anywhere near comparative to many other coaches who had failed, at one point he was actually working as a translator for a football manager.

No doubt he worked hard to get to where he is and achieve his success though many other people I am sure worked equally as hard if not harder without achieving his success. Was it his belief which made the difference, the extent of that we will never know though I am sure it didn't do him any harm.

Therefore you then need to find out from the expert what they are thinking and saying to themselves when they are performing at their best.

To find this out you will need to ask searching questions, once you have defined your successful model then you can transfer their skills and capabilities to yourself.

When implementing the model it is important to note the key steps.

Decide what skills and capabilities you want to model and the person/s that has these skills and capabilities.

1. Identify expert/s of the field and the ability to be modelled. (For example, public speaking, dancing, confidence in business, sport technique such as golf swing, football free kick.)

2. For each expert, gather information with respect to what and how s/he is thinking, feeling, believing and doing when manifesting the ability. (The Experiential Array and Belief Template are our information gathering tools.)

3. Use contrast and comparison of examples to identify the essential structural patterns for each expert.

4. Use contrast and comparison of experts to identify the essential structural patterns for the ability.

5. Test and refine the model.

Understanding the Modelling process

Each of us has a particular set of strategies which enables us to function effectively whilst performing sets of skills and capabilities, whether we are driving, cooking, playing sport, delivering a presentation, working in business and a thousand other functions. Yet these skills are most often acquired by unconscious trial and error. For example when you first learnt to drive your instructor taught you aspects of driving, when and how to change gears, rules of the road, and there may have been times you stalled the car, crunched the gears, drove slowly, got stuck in a traffic jam. Through your own experiences you learned and acquired a skill which is a similar process for most things we do e.g. delivering presentations, performing a task at work, participating in sport, because these skills are not obtained explicitly, we have little idea of how to transfer them to others.

What is more, people may excel using one particular strategy for a certain function, (playing a musical instrument, performing a task at work, a skill in sport) while seriously underachieving when they attempt to apply the same strategy elsewhere, (explaining the process of how they do what they do).

When you ask people who are really excellent, "How do you do it?" the most common response is, "I don't really know," or "I just... sort of... do it and everything happens naturally." This is typical of "unconscious competence". By the end of the modelling exercise the person being modelled invariably says, "Well, I never realised that's what I do," and often they will add, "I thought everyone did it that way!"

Even a little modelling will show that people often use widely different internal processing strategies, and this accounts for the gap between mediocre and top performers. Most strategies, once they are made explicit, can be easily learned or modified to accomplish organisational or personal goals.

When you have decided who you are going to model...

The first strategy is to model the expert on a physiological level.

Exercise

I.e. if you had to stand in for them to perform their skill how would you have to walk, talk?

Spend a few moments walking how they do and notice any insights into the expert's mind.

Write down any insights you gain by adopting their physiology and posture momentarily.

The Technique

Remember the five key points discussed earlier.

Decide what skills and capabilities you want to model and the person/s that has these skills and capabilities.

Questions to ask your expert:

Who was your inspiration? How did they inspire you?

Where and when do you perform your skill or capability?

What specifically do you do?

If you were going to teach me to do it, what would you ask me to do?

How did you learn to do this?

What do you believe about yourself when you do this?

Do you have a personal mission or vision when you do this?

How do you know you are good at this?

What emotional and physical state are you in when you do this?

What happened for you to be good at this?

What are you aiming to achieve when you're doing this? Who else do you recommend I talk to about this?

What may be useful; ask yourself the same questions and compare it to the ones of the model and decide what you can take from the model to boost and enhance your capabilities in a specific area.

Exercise

Ask yourself the same questions you have asked or elicited from your expert on the specific area you are modelling.

Who was your inspiration? How did they inspire you?

Where and when do you perform your skill or capability?

What specifically do you do?

If you were going to teach me to do it, what would you ask me to do?

How did you learn to do this?

What do you believe about yourself when you do this?

Do you have a personal mission or vision when you do this?

How do you know you are good at this?

What emotional and physical state are you in when you do this?

What happened for you to be good at this?

What are you aiming to achieve when you're doing this? Who else do you recommend I talk to about this?

Of course it is more useful if you can ask the questions at a first-hand interview. And I am sure you will be surprised as to who responds to you if you make the effort to contact your expert model, though if you're finding it difficult to obtain a response from the person/s you're looking to model read through interviews in magazines, on the Internet, in DVDs and access as much info as possible. It only takes one piece of information to make the difference to your life.

I am not advocating you are aiming to become that person as you will always keep your own unique identity as there is only one of you in the world. Though this is an opportunity to be able to access the mindsets of people who are already where you would like to be, and it can only be of benefit and assistance to learn how they did it and implement some of their strategies to your path to success.

Once you have elicited answers to the questions, with the invaluable insight you have gained from the model you can adapt these insights into you own mindset.

You can adapt the mechanics of the model's thought process at any level applicable to you helping you acquire these new skills and capabilities.

As a result this helps you gain a valuable insight of the difference that makes the difference. Put into action what you have learnt from the expert on every level, and attempt your skill or capability. Working with this template you can continue to refine the model and improve your skill level in this area keeping your own unique identity.

Take from the model key physiological movements; inherit some of the useful beliefs and mindset. Develop an action plan which integrates key skills the expert has acquired by practising and developing your ability as I am sure in becoming good at what your model expert does; they didn't wake up one morning and have a great golf swing, excellent communication skills, great sales skills, they worked at it by means of physical and mental practise, hiring a coach or trainer, developing a plan, which you can do too.

You can also use the power of your mind to reinforce, test and refine modelling these new skills and capabilities by using the following technique, which builds new neural pathways in the mind.

Technique

Exercise

1. Imagine being the expert in their field that you identified that has the behaviour, skills or abilities that you want for yourself.

2. Close your eyes and visualise that person in action. Watch it like a movie in your mind. See how they look, how they use their body, how they use their posture; how they stand, walk, and sit. Pay close attention. Hear how they talk, what they say, and how they say it.

3. See yourself as the model or yourself conducting this choice of behaviour skill or capability, you have stepped into the role model's place. You are watching yourself do as the model does. You have taken over the role and are acting exactly like your role model. Or imagine performing the skill or capability.

4. Do you feel any negativity come up within you when you watch yourself? Any doubts that you are capable of doing the skill or capability as the model does? Go through the actions of the skill, and adjust your action in the movie, until you are happy with how you perform the skill and capabilities; feel positive and confident in your abilities.

5. Mentally step inside the picture. You are now inside your movie image, looking through your own eyes. You are no longer watching yourself. You are doing the skill and capability just like the model does it. How does it feel to perform this skill or capability or be this person with these new skills and capabilities? How does your body feel?

How is your posture? What do you hear? How does your voice sound to you?

6. Imagine a future situation where you want to implement these skills and capabilities. Put yourself there. Look through your own eyes at this situation. You are the star of this movie and are behaving in the new way! Is it all working? Do you need to make any adjustments?

7. Open your eyes and come to the present moment.

8. Imagine that you are now the new you with these new capabilities. Get up and walk around as the new model. Walk the walk and talk the talk as they say. How does it feel?

The power of modelling is immense. To conclude the chapter I would like to share a time I was working with a team of aspiring young professional football players.

One of the players was short in stature and felt that this might be a factor in progressing in his career, as height was a key factor or seemed to be an important factor in the position and league he was playing.

I once read an autobiography by Roy Keane; one of the greatest midfielders of his generation, who I recalled mentioned something about his height and physical stature at a key point in his career and told the young player to read the book.

He told me he had read the book and it helped him to overcome certain beliefs he may have had about his height; this being a factor in gaining a professional career. This seemed to be a turning point in his career and he would go on to become an outstanding professional, he said if Roy Keane could do it so could he.

I am sure he learnt many other things from the autobiography and took what he felt necessary to take on board to create the leverage to break the belief barrier and become the best he could be.

Chapter 13: State of Mind, Getting in the Zone

Have you ever experienced being in the zone where everything seems to flow?

It could be delivering a presentation at work, a meeting, a game of golf with your friends, playing an instrument, where everything went exactly how you wanted it, almost as if in slow motion. Or a time you felt really confident, happy, motivated, for no specific reason you start to feel a certain way.

You could be driving to work in your car and a song comes on and it was the same song you heard on an amazing holiday a few years earlier and it brings back memories of what it was like, you start to feel relaxed, chilled, and happy.

Being in the right state of mind at the right time is crucial for success.

I recall a time I was driving in to BBC Radio 5 live to do an interview to discuss mental training. It was a Saturday evening and it had been a very long week. I had been travelling, delivering training and seminars all over the country and agreed to do the interview. I was driving in to the radio station.

I was told the broadcaster who was interviewing me was provocative and didn't buy into mental skills training. Added to that I knew 5 live was one of the highest listened to stations in the UK, and the show was accessible around the world.

I wasn't sure how to pitch the show because amongst the audience I figured there would be variable understanding of the mental skills concept so I wanted to ensure everyone could take something away from listening to the show. I arrived at the radio station I was ready and raring to go, only to be told my schedule was being put back an hour later. After being put back I recomposed myself only for my schedule to be put back again a further 30 minutes, it soon became very late at night, after a long week, with what was going to be a very provocative broadcaster.

As I finally sat down in my chair I could sense the broadcaster was going to make it as entertaining as possible with me being the source of entertainment. The provocation I was told would happen started, and after a long week, and the show being put back a couple of times I was feeling a bit tired.

My state of mind to say the least had altered from my enthusiasm I had upon arriving at the radio station.

Until I thought, I am here to discuss a subject I am passionate about, and I have the opportunity to help point many people in a positive direction. I needed to get myself in the zone and I did by doing a technique you will learn in this chapter. The show flowed and I received fantastic reviews, which would be the catalyst in unleashing my broadcasting career.

Before every show I did (and have done thereafter) I used the same technique, to get into the right frame of mind to deliver to the best of my ability. The mental aspects prior to performance should involve focusing on what you are going to do during the event and being in the right state of mind. Whether it is participating in top-flight sport, delivering a sales presentation, teaching a lesson to a group of students, going for a job interview, or meeting someone, being in right frame of mind at the right time is crucial.

In sport competition can bring out the best or the worst in athletes, and the psychological demands are especially high when individuals or teams are striving to achieve the same goals. When physical skills are evenly matched, it is often the competitor with the stronger mental approach, who can control his or her mind before and during events, who wins. Getting into the correct mindset prior to competition is one of the most crucial aspects of top performance.

In many ways life reflects competitive sport at the highest level, you have your ups and downs, sometimes you can feel you have no control of a situation, and life like sport can be an emotional roller coaster.

There are many other potential distractions for the sports person, just as there is for anybody playing in the game of life, including the actions of friends or family, coaches or teammates. The environmental conditions, memories, delays and irrelevant thoughts can all distract your focus. Having the ability to focus and be in the correct frame of mind to succeed in life and consistently produce results is important.

Many sports people and athletes have routines to get into the right state of mind.

Golfers have routines that allow them to prepare in the same way for each shot. Tennis players do before serving, as do some rugby place kickers (remember the image of Jonny Wilkinson, the famous England rugby kicker clenching his hands preparing to take a kick for goal). The key to any routine is that it provides the athlete with control and directs attention to the important cues. Coaches and athletes work together in deciding the key attention cues and the sequence in which these should occur.

A classic example of how emotions can affect sport performers came in a famous boxing match between Sugar Ray Leonard and Roberto Duran. Leonard was considered the better boxer and was expected to outclass Duran with slick movements and long-range punching. However, before the fight Duran insulted Leonard in front of his family and this, to the dismay of Leonard's trainer, Angelo Dundee, sent Leonard into a rage. This completely altered the course of subsequent events. Instead of fighting to the pre-planned strategy devised with his trainer Leonard let his emotions take over and decided he was going to "beat up" his opponent. Duran's actions amounted to a psychological master stroke as Leonard ditched his boxing skills and opted for a brawl. It was exactly what Duran had hoped for and he won a points decision.

The best performers in the world have the ability to get into the right state of mind in specific situations, particularly in certain situations where two competitors are equal physically, technically, and with their tactical understanding of the game. The ability that certain performers have to achieve consistent results over long periods of time has a lot to do with them being able to get in the right mental state in a specific situation.

Regardless of who you are and what you do, there are going to be times in your life where you encounter distractions and challenges and you need to be in the right frame of mind to deal with situations, whether you're a teacher, sales rep, delivering a presentation, want to ask some out on a date, attending a job interview or you have a task you want to complete.

A strategy I have used and use with many business people, sports people, people looking to find motivation and confidence at the right time is "Anchoring"; it is an NLP based technique which can be used to get anyone into the right state of mind.

You can change your state of mind or mood within an instant by using the anchoring technique. This means you can, for example, stay calm during that interview, relaxed during the meeting, confident during a presentation, motivated to go and exercise after a hard day, whatever is going on around you or however provocative a situation may be, you can stay focused and be in the right frame of mind.

What is Anchoring?

An anchor is a stimulus that creates a response in either you or in another person. When an individual is at the peak of an experience during an intense emotional state, an applied specific stimulus can establish a neurological link between the emotional state and the stimulus. Anchoring can occur naturally or be set up intentionally and can assist in gaining access to past states and linking the past state to the present and future. Anchors can be used by anyone to produce a state of mind or mood needed for a given situation.

Examples of how we develop an association to certain events:

→ Flicking through an old family photo album stirs pleasant memories and some of the feelings associated with them.

- An old song which can take you back to a specific event such as a memory of a holiday.
- The smell of freshly baked apple pies brings back memories of a happy carefree childhood.
- The smell of sunscreen reminding you of a relaxing holiday.
- A conversation with a friend you haven't seen for a while and reminiscing about the past.
- Driving past your old school.
- A tap on your shoulder or pat on your back.

How we anchor and are anchored

When we are with another person who experiences some strong emotion, whatever we are doing or saying becomes associated with that emotion. Usually this process occurs at the unconscious level. Subsequently, whenever we do or say the same thing in the same way in his/her presence we will tend to restimulate for him/her some portion of the previous feeling.

Being aware of this phenomenon through knowledge of neurolinguistic programming enables us to be aware of the kinds of responses we are anchoring in others, how we are doing it and conversely, what kinds of responses are being anchored in ourselves and how. This awareness enables us to anchor for mutually productive outcomes.

Anchoring is used in sport, business and personal development.

Can be used to create a resourceful state of mind for a specific situation to achieve a desired result.
- For example prior to a rugby player taking a kick for goal
- A golf player teeing off
- A cricket player getting ready to face the next ball

- A football player taking a penalty
- Delivering a presentation
- Attending a meeting
- Finding the motivation to exercise
- The confidence to ask someone out on a date
The list is limitless.

The anchor can be used to create different states of mind.

- Confidence
- Motivation
- Focus
- Relaxation

Examples

I was working with a leading football striker who was out of form and not performing due to spending a lot of time out injured and losing confidence; I had used the anchoring strategy by using technology. What we did was get as much video footage of the player performing to the best of his ability. The player's position in the team was to score goals. This was one of the outcomes he was aiming to achieve as a player. We transferred on to the DVD as many goals as possible, and there were quite a few. We then attached same of the player's favourite music to the DVD. Initially I had asked the player to take the DVD and watch it as and when he wanted to, just enjoy watching himself playing well. I said the fact he had performed like this before it was possible to perform like this again, it was a question of getting him in the same state of mind.

I then asked the player that in order to transfer this resource in a game situation we needed to develop an anchor. Just like a light switch we could switch that state of mind on when necessary. The player decided what he wanted to use an anchor was flicking his wristband. Whilst watching the DVD we went through the anchoring process hundreds of times until the player knew for certain that the anchor produced the emotional stimulus required for him to perform in specific situations we had outlined. The result was in the player's first game he scored two goals and had his best season thereafter.

Another example of the anchoring process was some work I did with a football player at a lower division club. In this situation I did not have access to video footage of the player. So we did the process by getting the player to reflect on some of his past performances. The player was going through a situation where he was lacking in confidence, whenever he walked on to the football pitch he didn't believe in himself. This player also being a striker, whose job it is to score goals, was doing well in training, he had no problem scoring goals in training, though when he walked on to the football pitch, he couldn't seem to score goals. The reasons behind this could have been countless, and I thought that it isn't necessary to find out why. Rather than analyse the problem let's look for a solution. The player was going through a problem where he was lacking confidence whilst he was playing a competitive game, which was affecting his performances. We went through the anchoring process; I asked him to sit down and write down some of his best performances. Having done this you could see an immediate physiological change, the player sat up straight his breathing changed and almost in an instant was in a different mindset. We decided on an anchor, which was a flick of his wristband aimed at associating the action to high levels of confidence. I asked him to visualise again his best performances.

As soon as he associated to the state of confidence he wanted to recreate, and when the feelings had reached peak intensity I asked him to flick his wristband as this would build an association to the confidence he wanted as a resource whilst playing. Every time he wanted to tap in to that resource he would flick his wristband. The player performed the technique and practiced whilst on his own and the first thing he does when he walks on to the pitch now is flick the wristband. This had a positive impact on his performances, helping him to become one of the team's and league's top players.

I also developed team anchors. I was working with a football team that was struggling, and they were bottom of the league and heading for relegation. I developed a team anchor which was a huddle before the match. I played a DVD of their best performance and the significance and association of a team anchor, which was the huddle, was to approach each game with exactly the same level of application and effort. The team went on to win 8 out of 10 of their last games and survived relegation against all odds. Every game they played after developing the anchor was outstanding.

Other things I use anchoring for are business people delivering presentations, meetings, sales reps, helping people switch on motivation and confidence. And also other sports such as golf and cricket when there is a break in play where you need to focus at the right time.

Installing an Anchor Exercise:

1. Decide on a specific event that you wish to access a particular state of mind (confidence, motivation) for, e.g. a presentation, interview, or meeting.

2. Decide on the state you want to anchor – e.g. being calm and relaxed, confident, motivated, etc.

3. Choose an anchor (or anchors) that you wish to use to trigger that state – e.g. press thumb and middle finger together; flick wristband.

4. Recall a memory or imagine a situation where you can experience that state – e.g. recall a situation where you were totally calm, relaxed, confident, etc.; and fully associate to that memory or feeling. Close your eyes and notice what you saw, felt, heard.

5. When the experience is vivid and you are in the desired state, follow the desire through to the peak of its intensity, then squeeze your thumb and middle finger together; flick your wristband.

6. Release the anchor(s) when the experience begins to fade.

7. Now do something else – open your eyes, count down from 10 to break the state and distract yourself.

Repeat the steps above several times, each time trying to make the memory more vivid (not required when the anchor is established at the high point of a real experience, but you can strengthen the anchor by establishing it at the high point of several such experiences).

8. Apply the anchor and check that the required state occurs.

9. Future pace and imagine your forthcoming event using your anchor.

KEYS TO ANCHORING

INTENSITY of the experience

An anchor should be applied when you are fully associated in an intense state. The more intense the experience, the better the anchor will connect.

TIMING of the anchor

When you reach the beginning of the state, apply the anchor. When you reach its peak, let it go. This can vary typically from five to fifteen seconds. For example if you're anchoring confidence as soon as you're reliving a time you were confident apply the anchor as soon as you first have the feelings and release just as you reach peak.

STACK the anchor

The anchor has to be repeated and reinforced in the same way from time to time. Every time you receive praise, recognition, stack your anchor to reinforce the positive feelings.

NUMBER of times

Repetition of the stimulus, the number of times the stimulus is applied. The more often, the more powerful the anchor will be. If you keep adding, or stacking anchors, it becomes even more powerful.

You now have a powerful technique to help you get the best out of yourself in any situation.

Another way to get into a resourceful state of mind almost immediately is mindset.

NLP Physiology Strategies

Have you ever come across the type of person who walks with their head down, back hunched, talks slowly, and trudges around? On the other hand what about the type of person that walks with purpose, head up, shoulders back with a sense of direction?

Many years ago the first person was me. Growing up I lacked a lot of confidence and I didn't excel at school. Growing up I was always small in height and struggled to compete with my peers in sport. My height and stature made it difficult for me growing up because I matured very late physically, I would almost hide with my head down, back hunched, to avoid being pushed around. Even when I grew to over 6 feet I still walked around with my head down, trudging along, it wasn't until I learnt a NLP technique called Walk with Grace and Power, that I worked with my posture and with that came a transformation of my confidence.

One of the points I stress with the athletes, sports people and footballers I work with is to adopt a confident positive posture. Whether they are standing side by side with the opposition in the tunnel getting ready to walk on to the pitch or have given everything on a sports field with a few minutes to go, keep a positive confident posture.

I recall a few years ago working with a professional footballer who was on the opposition team against the team I was working with a couple years earlier. He said at half-time they felt physically knackered in what was a thrilling encounter. When they walked out in the second half and they saw the team I was working with standing tall, shoulders back, heads up, he said his team was literally beaten at that point.

Just to set the scene; if you were a student and you saw your teacher walk in with purpose, or you were interviewing someone who walked in with shoulders back, or someone steps up to deliver a presentation with self-assurance, what would your impressions be?

I recall once being back in Sydney, Australia, delivering seminars. I hadn't been back to Australia in many years and it was where I was born and grew up. I wasn't sure how the audience would respond to my seminars. There was a little bit of uncertainty in my mind, as the seminars were well publicised on the radio and in the papers, and there I was ready to stand up. I thought at that point, the best way to get into the right state is walk out with a sense of purpose head up shoulders back, and the seminars went down like a storm.

By changing the way you move your body, you can have a subtle but important influence on the way you feel.

Here's a quick experiment to illustrate this point:

1. Try to feel depressed as you jump up and down and shake your hands in the air

2. Try to feel confident as you slump your shoulders and look down

3. Try to feel tired and listless as you march around the room

Changing your physiology is probably the simplest way to change your frame of mind in an instant.

The technique is something you can work on, practise for a few minutes a day correcting your posture, bringing your shoulders back, back straight and head up, get in front of a mirror, and work on your walking.

Exercise

Step 1: Stand up straight in front of a mirror

Step 2: Put your shoulders back with your head held high

Step 3: Stand in that position for one minute

Step 4: Walk in that position, practise pacing

Step 5: Whilst pacing in your position of power and confidence, focus on five of your best qualities

Notice how you begin to feel, even after a minute. When you perfect this technique, it is something that will occur naturally and give you a sense of pride in who you are.

Chapter 14: Time Out

"A good rest is half the work."

Proverb

Could you imagine living in a world without a television, a mobile phone, computer, the Internet, no deadlines at work, no need to be at a certain place at a certain time? You only have to take a trip to the local shopping centre and you notice people on their mobile phones, talking, texting, rushing around to get to one place and another. Whilst there are many benefits of modern technology and the modern world we live in, the one thing we are probably all guilty of is not giving ourselves the opportunity to unwind. And by unwinding I am not just referring to an annual holiday, which sometimes can be a stressful adventure in itself. How many of us on a daily basis take the opportunity to switch off and relax, meditate, and kick back? Switch everything off, no TVs, no phones, nowhere you have to be, even for 10 minutes, just letting things go and relaxing. Unlike our ancestors, we live with constant stress. Instead of occasional, acute demands followed by rest, we're constantly overworked, undernourished, exposed to environmental toxins, worrying about others, we are working longer hours, placing more demands on ourselves — with no let up, which in turn leads to a stressful lifestyle. A certain level of stress is fine, as it can motivate us to do things, though high levels of stress can be damaging to people's health. The effects of stress can produce high levels of cortisol in the body. This can cause illness. Studies and research have proven by adopting relaxation strategies we can bring down our levels of cortisol, improve our well-being, and bring down our heart rate and blood pressure.

What is cortisol? In its normal function, cortisol helps us meet these challenges by converting proteins into energy, releasing glycogen and counteracting inflammation. For a short time, that's okay, but at sustained high levels, cortisol gradually tears your body down.

Sustained high cortisol levels destroy healthy muscle and bone, slow down healing and normal cell regeneration, co-opt biochemicals needed to make other vital hormones, impair digestion, metabolism and mental function, interfere with healthy endocrine function and weaken your immune system.

Cortisol is an important hormone in the body, secreted by the adrenal glands and involved in the following functions and more:

→ Proper glucose metabolism
→ Regulation of blood pressure
→ Insulin release for blood sugar maintenance
→ Immune function
→ Inflammatory response

However prolonged high levels of cortisol can lead to heart disease and other health problems. Just think of your body's response when you watch a part in a scary film, or when you receive some bad news, you're frightened, upset, or embarrassed. Notice what happens to your physiology in times of stress, your heart beats faster, palms get clammy, and nerves in your stomach get tingly.

This is the body's response to perceived threat or danger. During this reaction, certain hormones like adrenalin and cortisol are released, speeding the heart rate, slowing digestion, shunting blood flow to major muscle groups, and changing various other autonomic nervous functions, giving the body a burst of energy and strength. Originally named for its ability to enable us to physically fight or run away when faced with danger. When we first evolved it was a response to perceived danger; people would either fight or run. Though the dangers the first humans faced are no doubt different to the ones we have now, technology may have of evolved, our human responses are similar, fight or flight is now activated in situations where neither response is appropriate, like in a traffic jam or during a stressful day at work. When the perceived threat is gone, systems are designed to return to normal function via the relaxation response, but in our times of chronic stress, this often doesn't happen enough, causing damage to the body.

Small increases of cortisol have some positive effects like helping us:

- ➜ Kick into action on a Monday morning
- ➜ Get our brain in gear before an exam
- ➜ With a burst of energy when we are tired
- ➜ Lower sensitivity to pain if we have an accident
- ➜ In sport, producing bursts of effort

To keep cortisol levels healthy and under control, the body's relaxation response should be activated after the fight or flight response occurs. So after a stress full day at work, when you feel overwhelmed or upset you take a time out during the day to recharge the batteries. Also make lifestyle changes creating a balance, so you're not having to face stressful situations frequently, such as going out for country walks, spending time doing activities which relax you and take your mind off stressful situations.

The following strategy is one I use with athletes and business people I work with to help them relax after stressful times in their lives. By reducing the stress not only are there health benefits, there are the benefits of improved performance, feeling sharper, more focused and positive.

Experiment

To signify the power of relaxation physiologically with my clients I ask them to take their pulse rate over a minute.

And retake their pulse rate after a relaxation exercise. Significantly their pulse rate drops sometimes up to 20 beats per minute, just with a 15 to 20 minute relaxation script. The significance of 20 beats per minutes is if you think of how many minutes we have in a day, times 20, so that's thousands of beats less strain per day on your heart.

So take your heart rate before the script by finding your pulse on your wrist, or on your neck, and count how many beats it completes in a minute. Then at the end of the relaxation strategy take your pulse rate again and notice the difference in your heart rate.

Relaxation Exercise

You can record the following script and play it back to yourself with relaxing music playing in the background.

Closing your eyes, take a deep breath in and breathe out, clear your mind out. Imagine emptying all your thoughts into a bag and leaving it in a place you can pick it up in a short time if you wish. As you empty your mind, imagine visiting a place where you feel completely relaxed and at ease. It could be a peaceful holiday destination, an amazing beach, it could be a relaxing countryside walk, or you could imagine lying back on a yacht which is sailing on a beautiful river or crystal-clear ocean, you feel happy, secure, and loved. It's a beautiful day, the sky is a special shade of blue, very clear and it's a warm day, a warm summer's day. The sun is shining brightly. You close your eyes and feel the warmth of the sun on your back.

You feel the warmth of the sun on every muscle in your body, you feel a gentle breeze on your face, and you feel at peace and at ease with the world. As you feel the warmth of the sun on your back, the warmth spreads to your shoulders and arms, you begin to relax even deeper, and this relaxing warmth is spreading further throughout every muscle in your body.

Move the warmth from the sun into your hands, feel the warmth of the light from the sun in your palms, relax all those muscles, let go, feel at ease and peaceful. The warmth of the sun moves into your legs relaxing your thighs, and the warmth, spreading to the backs of your legs, makes them feel relaxed.

You feel completely relaxed, so comfortable and at peace with the world. And you direct the warmth of the sun down the from the back of your thighs, into your calf muscles, the warmth of the sun releasing tension and stress from every muscle in your legs into your feet, to the tips of your toes, you feel the warmth of the sun, relaxing you.

As you breathe in you inhale crystal-clear relaxing air, and you exhale all your stresses and strains. As you hear yourself breathing and you feel your heart beating, you becoming more and more relaxed.

Inhale fresh energising air, and exhaling all your stresses and strains, you release all your stresses and strains, feeling more and more relaxed. As you feel the warmth of the sun all over every muscle in your body you exhale every last bit of stress. You carry on inhaling fresh energising air spreading into every cell in your body feeling completely relaxed. Your whole body is now totally and completely relaxed, from the top of your head to the tips of your toes. As your body relaxes, so does your mind. As your mind relaxes just notice the sun going down, going down and down, deeper and deeper. The sky is ablaze with an abundance of colours of crimson and bright purple and blue yellow streaks. It's a beautiful summer's evening – your mind relaxes and lets go, releases all the stresses of the day. You feel safe, secure, at peace. You seize the moment, and take it all in; you pick up a refreshing drink, refreshing every part of your body.

As you watch the sun go down, you notice a clear summer night's sky with the stars twinkling, millions of stars twinkling in the summer night's sky, you notice one particular shining star; you focus completely on that star.

Nothing else matters except this beautiful, single, solitary, sparkling star in the sky. It's a beautiful summer's night. You feel so safe, secure, so comfortable, relaxed, happy and at peace with the universe.

Imagine yourself now, floating towards that star in the sky, moving up, and up and up. Your body is weightless as it lifts you up to the star, going higher and higher, up and up. As you look down you notice all the bright lights shining down below, an amazing view, you can see all your family and friends happy and relaxed. You are completely at ease. You now float to touching distance of the star, you reach out, you become the star and the star is you. You are one, back from where you came. It's a beautiful star. So you go deeper and deeper relaxed. Just let your mind go, you are at peace, calm, happy and relaxed. Let your mind and body relax and experience the joy of pure relaxation at the deepest level.

Gradually now, when you're ready to come back to the here and now in your own time...

Completely refreshed, relaxed, recharged and re-energised, on the count of 5 you come back to the here and now...

Completely refreshed, relaxed, recharged and re-energised, with an understanding of your life's path and purpose...

5... Gradually coming round...
4... Feeling refreshed, relaxed...
3... Recharged, revitalized...
2... Feeling rejuvenated, relaxed, recharged...
1...

Back to the here and now:

Completely refreshed, relaxed, recharged and re-energised.

"Every now and then go away, have a little relaxation, for when you come back to your work your judgment will be surer.. Go some distance away because then the work appears smaller and more of it can be taken in at a glance and a lack of harmony and proportion is more readily seen."

Leonardo De Vinci

In the next chapter we will focus on the Power of Visualisation and Imagery.

Chapter 15: The Power of Visualisation and Imagery

At one point the house you live in, the car you drive, the phone you use will have all been a part of someone's imagination. Our mind is capable of producing positive and negative thoughts and images.

This chapter will help you focus on how you want things to go, overcome fears, phobias, become more focused, and achieve excellence, overcome challenges and obstacles.

The mind cannot distinguish the difference between reality and "non-reality". Have you ever had a bad dream and woke up in the middle of the night, with your heart racing? Or watched a scary film which got your pulse racing?

In sport, athletes use visualisation to focus on how they want the outcome of a race or training session to go, or to keep calm before the nerves of a big event kick in, or after a competition when the adrenalin has been pumping throughout an event or competition, to be able to rest in a relaxed feeling of calm and well-being. By imagining a scenario, complete with images of a previous best performance or a future desired outcome, the athlete is able to get themselves in the correct state of mind by vividly imagining the process they want to perform and the outcome at the end of the event. This helps the athlete stay relaxed, focused and confident.

Research has found in sport that visualisation can have a big impact in performance. Visualisation and imagery can give the athlete the confidence to perform certain skills under high pressure situations, or in a variety of possible situations. The most effective visualisation techniques result in a very vivid sport experience in which the athlete has complete control over a successful performance.

Research carried out at the University of Chicago into visualisation in basketball players divided a number of people into three groups. Each was tested shooting a number of penalty shots in basketball. The groups were then given different instructions:

→ Group 1 did not practice penalty shots for 30 days;
→ Group 2 practiced shots every day for 30 days;
→ Group 3 practiced shots only in their mind (visualisation) for 30 days.

After 30 days the three groups were tested again:

→ Group 1 showed no improvement at all (as expected);
→ Group 2 showed a 24% improvement (not especially satisfactory given that they had been practicing with the ball for one month);
→ Group 3 improved by 23% (impressive considering they had not even seen a ball for 30 days!).

Similar techniques using similar principles can help people be at the best for everyday life, both personally and professionally.

To prepare for an interview, deliver a presentation, overcome stressful and anxious situations, build confidence in interacting with people, approaching someone you're attracted to; with mental rehearsal, minds and bodies become trained to actually perform the skill imagined and give the best possible chance to achieve an outcome.

In sport these scenarios can include any of the five senses. They can be visual (images and pictures), kinaesthetic (how the body feels), auditory (the roar of the crowd), smell (of the freshly cut grass), or taste (of sports drink before match). Using the mind, athletes call up these images over and over, enhancing the skill through repetition or rehearsal, similar to physical practice.

A similar process can be used for anybody looking to focus on a positive outcome whether it is recreating an interview, presentation, meeting, phone call, or a pleasant day. Create a mental image or intention of what you want to happen or feel.

Imagery can be shown to work by using biofeedback devices that measure body stress. By imagining pleasant and unpleasant scenes, you can actually see or hear the levels of stress in your body change.

How do we visualise?

First, let's get a better understanding of how the process works, by using one of the key aspects, what we call in NLP Sub modalities.

What are Modalities and Sub Modalities?

It is important to note we process and learn information through our senses. We have five basic senses: visual sight, auditory sound, kinaesthetic feelings, olfactory smell and gustatory taste. For each of these modalities, we can have finer distinctions. We could describe a picture as being black and white or colour, or it could also be bright or dim. Sounds could be loud or soft, or coming from a particular direction. Feelings could be in different parts of the body or have different temperatures. Smells could be pleasant or offensive, strong or light. Taste could be sweet or bitter or strong or mild. These finer distinctions are called sub modalities and define the qualities of our internal representations. Most people work with only three modalities – visual (see), auditory (hear) and kinaesthetic (feel). However olfactory (smell) or gustatory (taste) sub modalities can play an important part of some people's association to experience.

Some of the more common sub modalities are:

- ➤ Visual/Auditory/Kinaesthetic
- ➤ Black & White or Colour
- ➤ Near or Far
- ➤ Bright or Dim
- ➤ Location
- ➤ Size of Picture
- ➤ Associated/Dissociated
- ➤ Focused or Defocused
- ➤ Framed or Unbounded
- ➤ Movie or Still
- ➤ If a Movie: Fast/Normal/Slow
- ➤ Dimensional or Flat. Loud or Soft
- ➤ Near or Far
- ➤ Internal or External
- ➤ Stereo or Mono
- ➤ Fast or Slow
- ➤ High or Low Pitch
- ➤ Verbal or Tonal
- ➤ Rhythm
- ➤ Clarity
- ➤ Pauses: Strong or Weak

- ➜ Large Area or Small Area
- ➜ Weight: Heavy or Light
- ➜ Texture: Smooth or Rough
- ➜ Constant or Intermittent
- ➜ Temperature: Hot or Cold
- ➜ Size
- ➜ Shape
- ➜ Pressure
- ➜ Vibration

The visual sub modality Associated/Dissociated is very important and refers to whether or not you can see yourself in the picture (visual internal representation). You are associated if you cannot see yourself in the picture, you are experiencing the event. Often we refer to this as "looking through your own eyes". If you can see yourself in the picture, then we say you are dissociated for example watching a television.

If you are associated in a memory, then your feelings (happy, sad, and fearful) about that memory will be more intense. If you are dissociated, this is more like watching a movie of your life rather than being there (on the playing field) and any feelings will be less intense.

Exercise 1

The following four exercises illustrate how sub modalities work. Close your eyes think of a recent experience e.g. driving in to work, walking to the shop. Notice any images in your mind (an internal representation). For some people, the pictures we make in our minds are very clear. For others the picture won't be as clear, which is why it is important whilst we use imagery we associate to other senses which people might have stronger association to.

Exercise 2

Get in a comfortable position, close your eyes and get a picture in your mind of a pleasant experience, e.g. a holiday, family meal. When you get this picture, notice the sub modalities. Is it a bright or dim picture, what feelings do you have, any sounds, do you recall any music, conversations, any smells e.g. the beach, sunscreen, any tastes, where are the sights, sounds, feelings located, are you associated reliving the experience, or dissociated like watching it on TV, etc.? Once you have done this, open your eyes and clear your mind by stretching and looking around the room. Clear your mind of that experience.

Exercise 3

Again close your eyes and this time get a picture in your mind of a mildly unpleasant experience. Notice the sub modalities i.e. what you see, hear, feel. Any smells? Tastes? Of this experience, can you identify several that are different from the picture of an enjoyable experience? Once you have done this, clear your focus by stretching and looking around the room.

I am sure you were able to identify several sub modalities that were different in the two internal representations.

Generally, we tend to have similar sub modalities for the internal representations for pleasant experiences. The sub modalities of the internal representations of unpleasant experiences will also be similar sub modalities and in some way different from the sub modalities of pleasant experiences. This sameness and difference in sub modalities allows us to code our experiences and give meaning to our past and future memories (internal representations).

Did you notice the proximity of both experiences, of where they're large, up close (i.e. "in your face"), what do you think would happen if you made the picture smaller and pushed it away to a comfortable distance? It would make the intensity of the experience less significant.

Exercise 4

For this exercise, I would like you to close your eyes and think of a time when you were very happy. Once you have this picture, make it very dark, shrink it down to a small picture and push it far away. When you did this, what did you notice about your feelings of happiness? Reduced or disappeared? You have just learned a great way to remove happiness from your life – take all your happy memories and make the pictures very dark, small and far away. Of course, I am joking. However, there are some people who tend to discount their happy memories by making them darker, smaller and further away, while making their unpleasant memories big and bright and close. And how do you think they live their lives?

These two examples illustrate that the sub modalities you use to store your memories (past and future) give meaning to your memories. We cannot change an event that has already happened, however by adjusting the sub modalities of the memory we can change how we perceive it and respond to it. This is also true for future events.

Sub modalities: Key Building Blocks of NLP Techniques

Story

I recall my first experience of working with an offender, I read the case file to get an idea of the person I would be working with and made my way in the car to the appointment. As I was driving I felt assured in the knowledge I had done a significant amount of training and was fully prepared and trained, though what kept running through my mind is what I read on the offender's file, which described the offender's behaviour and other relevant details. I imagined someone who was six foot five; something like out of a Texas chainsaw massacre film. I kept driving and these images kept running through my mind and slowly I could feel my pulse rising, palms sweaty, and I was imagining all sorts of scenarios. I put a range of CDs on to psyche myself up, various rock compilations and I still felt an element of nerves. I arrived at my destination and was introduced to various staff. I was then greeted by the person I was meant to be working with. As they appeared he was around five foot one and the complete opposite in stature and character to what I imagined. How many times does our mind's perception of an event or situation produce distorted images, sounds, feelings, smells, tastes, to what the experience actually turns out to be?

Almost like going to a party you are not sure about going to, and you end up having a good time. Or the opposite can happen. Or you get called in by the boss at work and you start imagining the worst. You are thinking about approaching someone on a date, and you have a flash of different things running through your mind. It's important we take control of our mind and don't let our mind control us. Before we go on to techniques and strategies to overcome any anxiety, fears and phobia let's look further into sub modalities.

Sub modalities are key components to many of the NLP change techniques.

Sub modalities, by themselves or as part of other techniques have been used to assist people to stop smoking, eat more of certain foods and less of others, address compulsion issues, change beliefs and values, enhance motivation, move from stress to relaxation, address phobias, etc.

By changing an internal image, feeling, voice; if you are bothered by an internal image, feeling, voice that limits you in some way, then:

- ➔ Change the colour of the image
- ➔ Push the image away
- ➔ Release some of the negative feelings
- ➔ Turn down the volume
- ➔ Make it more pleasant
- ➔ Make it appear to come from farther away

The following is a technique to help you release a phobia, overcome a fear:

I have used this technique to help people overcome many fears and phobias, such as fear of delivering presentations, meetings, and flying, driving on motorways, the list is endless. The following technique can help you overcome fears and phobias you may have.

There have been times I have worked with clients who have had phobias for several years, I have used this technique which takes around 20-30 minutes and they have overcome their fear or phobia, never to look back again.

Fast Phobia Cure – The Technique

It only takes an instant to develop a fear or a phobia. For example, an instant of turbulence in a plane, a negative comment at an interview, a flat presentation, an incident on the motorway.

However, as quick as we incur the fear or phobia, we can just as quickly overcome it, by using the power of association and sub modalities.

The following is the technique, a step-by-step guide to help you overcome a fear or a phobia.

1. Find and confront your fear or phobia in your mind's eye.
2. Imagine walking into an "imaginary" movie theatre of the mind and sit down in the centre of the front row.
3. Imagine floating up out of your body and gently settling in a comfortable seat in the balcony, so you can watch yourself watching the screen.
4. Put the very beginning of your phobia on the screen in the form of a coloured slide. Run the movie of your phobia all the way to end, as you remain in the balcony watching sitting in the front row watching yourself on the screen.
5. At the end of the movie, freeze the frame into a slide. Change the picture to black and white and then reassociate fully into the picture on the screen ("walk into the movie"). Run the associated movie backwards at triple speed or faster, with circus or cartoon music playing, and have them freeze-frame the image when they get to the beginning of the movie.

6. Walk out of the still picture and sit back down in the centre of the front row of the theatre, then white out the entire screen.

7. Repeat steps 3-6 as necessary. Test for the phobic response after each time through.

The critical point is the dissociation from the actual event. When association is eventually imposed, it is so bizarre that the brain rewrites the memory and unlearns the phobia as quickly as it learnt it. Technically this is a brain reimprinting exercise and this is best explained in a little story.

Imagine you are walking down a road and come to a dead end. In front of you is a large cornfield with corn grown to shoulder height. You cannot see the sides of this field nor can you see the other side. The corn is growing right up to the fence so it is not possible to walk round the field, so you decide to walk straight across the field. It takes quite some endeavour to trample your way across the field but with time and effort you succeed to getting to the other side. Job done.

Next day you arrive at the end of the same road and have the same task in front of you (to get to the other side) this time it is much easier as all you have to do is follow your tracks from yesterday. This pattern is then repeated day after day.

So we see from this example that the first time you do something you carve new neural pathways in your brain and this takes some energy to do. When subjected to the same or similar situation again you will have the tendency to go down the same (neural) pathway. This tendency is reinforced time after time until it becomes a habit or phobic response.

Therefore to break the habit or phobic response you need to carve a new neural pathway(s) or go down a different path. The NLP fast phobia cure does just that. It helps you to create a new pathway, a pathway that does not include an unsuitable response to a given situation; i.e. a phobia.

The Imagination

Advocates of imagery, contend that the imagination is a potent healer that has long been overlooked by practitioners of Western medicine. Imagery can relieve pain, speed healing and help the body subdue hundreds of ailments, including depression, impotence, allergies and asthma.

Imagery is the most fundamental language we have. Everything you do, the mind processes through images. When we recall events from our past or childhood, we think of pictures, images, sounds, pain, etc. It is hardly ever through words.

As discussed, images aren't necessarily limited to visuals but can be sounds, tastes, smells or a combination of sensations. A certain smell, for example, may invoke either pleasant or bad memories in you. Similarly, going to a place where you had a bad accident may instantly invoke visions of the accident and initiate a flight or fight response.

Think, for example, of holding a fresh, juicy lemon in your hand. Perhaps you can feel its texture or see the vividness of its yellow skin. As you slice it open, you see the juice squirt out of it. The lemon's aroma is overwhelming. Finally, you begin to eat the lemon and chew the lemon, and taste the sour flavour as the juices roll over your tongue.

More than likely, your body reacted in some way to that image. For example, you may have begun to salivate.

Imagery Can Involve Negative Visualisations too

Unfortunately, many of the images popping into our heads do more harm than good. In fact, the most common type of imagery is worry, because when we worry, what we worry about exists only in our imaginations.

It is estimated that an average person has 10,000 thoughts or images flashing through their mind each day. At least half of those thoughts are negative, such as the anxiety of meeting a quota, a coming speech, job-related anxiety, etc. Unharnessed, a steady dose of worry and other negative images can alter your physiology and make you more susceptible to a variety of ailments, ranging from acne to arthritis, headaches to heart disease, and ulcers to urinary tract infections.

Your thoughts have a direct influence on the way you feel and behave. If you tend to dwell on sad or negative thoughts, you most likely are not a very happy person. Likewise, if you think that your job is enough to give you a headache, you probably will come home with throbbing temples each day. This is just another clear example of the power the mind exerts over the body.

But if you can learn to direct and control the images in your head, you can help your body heal itself. Our imagination is like a spirited, powerful horse. If it's untamed, it can be dangerous and run you over, but if you learn to use your imagination in a way that is purposeful and directed, it can be a tremendously powerful vehicle to get you where you want to go, including to better health.

Your imagination can be a powerful tool to help you combat stress, tension, and anxiety. You can use visualisation to harness the energy of your imagination, and it does not take long – probably just a few weeks – to master the technique. Try to visualise two or three times a day. Most people find it easiest to do in bed in the morning and at night before falling asleep, though with practice you'll be able to visualise whenever and wherever the need arises.

How Effective is Imagery?

Imagery has been found to be very effective for the treatment of stress. Imagery is at the centre of relaxation techniques designed to release brain chemicals that act as your body's natural brain tranquillisers, lowering blood pressure, heart rate, and anxiety levels. By and large, research has found that these techniques work. Because imagery relaxes the body, imagery is often recommended for stress-related conditions such as headaches, chronic pain in the neck and back, and high blood pressure.

A test you can do yourself which illustrates the power of imagery when you do the relaxation technique later in this chapter.

One of the tests I ask my clients to do is as follows. I ask them to take their heart rate; how many beats per minute prior to a relaxation strategy. After 15 to 20 minutes of relaxation and imagery retake their heart rate and write down how many beats per minute.

In my experience I have noted some clients' heart rates come down as much as 20 beats per minute, which might not sound a lot though, if you multiply 20 times as many minutes in a day that is thousands of beats less stress on your heart per day.

In my experience I found imagery works best when it is used in conjunction with a relaxation technique. When your physical body is relaxed, you don't need to be in such conscious control of your mind, and you can give it the freedom to daydream, sit back and relax and let everything go.

Relaxation Exercise before Imagery:

Imagine emptying all your thoughts into a bag and putting it to one side, you can always pick these thoughts up later, though for now relax. Imagine walking down a staircase and as you take one step at a time you become more and more relaxed, carry on walking down till you become totally relaxed.

Imagine opening a door and as you open a door, imagine walking into a favourite scene. It could be a beach, a mountain, or a particularly enjoyable moment with friends or family. Try to go into this scene each time you practice your imagery. If you can create a special, safe place where nothing can hurt you and you feel secure, it will make you more receptive to other images.

Once you feel comfortable in your favourite scene, gradually direct your mind to an event you want to rehearse, keeping focused.

Focusing on how you want things to develop working towards your outcome.

Imagery and Visualisation

Your thoughts have a direct influence on the way you feel and behave. If you tend to dwell on sad or negative thoughts, you most likely are not a very happy person.

Your imagination can be a powerful tool to help you combat stress, tension, and anxiety; focus on what you want. You can use visualisation to harness the energy of your imagination, and it can have an impact right away, the more you do it the better you will get. Get into the habit of using visualisation and imagery to help you overcome life's challenges.

Relaxation Technique Tips

(To be used before Visualisation)
To begin visualisation, sit down in a comfortable position and close your eyes. Just let everything go and completely relax. Relax every part of your body.

➜ Starting from your toes, flex your toes and relax
➜ Moving up to your ankles, flex and relax
➜ Working your way up every muscle in your body, tense your calves release and relax
➜ Your muscles at the front of your legs your quads and at the back of your legs, your hamstrings, tense and relax

Inhaling and exhaling gently, imagine breathing out stress in the form of black smoke, and inhaling a relaxing clear energy, relaxing your lower back, chest, neck, facial muscles, eyes, and relax your mind. As you relax your mind, imagine emptying all your thoughts in a bin liner.

As you empty your thoughts you free your mind, knowing you can pick up any thoughts if you wish later, though for now, just let go and relax. Once you feel relaxed, begin thinking of a time when you felt happy, peaceful, calm, and in tune with the world. Imagine every aspect of the time, the place, the people, the sounds, colours, feelings, involving all of your senses, you are now at peace and in tune with the world, open to opportunities.

It is important to use all five senses. For example: if you like to visualise waves crashing on a beach, imagine first what this looks like: the waves crashing on the shore, the waves moving in from the seas, the size and movement of the waves, the sky above and the sun filtering through the sun sparkling on the ocean. Then imagine the smell of the sea, sunscreen, and barbeque in the distance. Next listen for the sounds the waves crashing on the shore, children laughing and playing in the distance, the breeze blows, birds singing. How does the sand feel beneath your feet? Soft and smooth and warm, the gentle sun on your glowing back, gentle breeze blowing on your face. Imagine drinking a cool drink quenching your thirst. As you become more involved in your visual image, your body will relax and you will be able to let go of the problems or worries that you'd felt before. To encourage this relaxation to occur, you can punctuate the images with positive statements, such as "I feel loved and secure" or "I feel calm and relaxed".

The following are some imagery scripts to assist you with some of life's challenges.

Using imagery to prepare for presentations

To begin, choose a comfortable position, seated or lying down. Make sure that you have no distractions around you and are not trying to do anything besides focusing on these words and allowing yourself to become relaxed.

Get comfortable, preparing to relax. Start to relax your body. Take a deep breath in... and breathe out. In and out. Continue to breathe deeply, slowly, and comfortably.

Count down now, from 10... to... 1. As you count each number, you can become more relaxed.

Let's begin.

10 Let your muscles start to relax
9 The tips of your toes are warming and relaxing spreading gently through your body...
8 Your muscles are becoming more and more relaxed...
7 Notice your mind drifting... becoming more relaxed...
6 Relax even further now letting everything go... feeling peaceful...
5 ...A warm feeling of relaxation and love spreading through your body... pleasant and relaxed
4 ...becoming more and more relaxed and peaceful, tranquil...
3 ...free your mind to relax...
2 ...feeling completely relaxed...
1 ...you are now in a deep state of relaxation.

You are very deeply relaxed, comfortable, loved, secure and happy.

Allow this feeling of relaxation to grow... becoming even more relaxed... calm and peaceful.

Keep with you the feeling of relaxation, love and security as you think about public speaking. Notice your reaction, physically and emotionally, to the concept of public speaking. Perhaps in the past this has been a source of anxiety for you... notice now how you can be relaxed, calm and confident while thinking about speaking in public.

Calm, relaxed, confident. Peaceful and relaxed.

In the future you will know that the stress symptoms you may experience when faced with speaking publicly indicate excitement. This is a positive feeling, filling you with energy. The thought of speaking in front of people fills you with good feelings of excitement and anticipation.

You may even be feeling a bit excited now, just thinking about public speaking. Let this feeling subside as you return to a state of deep relaxation.

Take a deep breath in... Hold... and exhale.

Breathe in... and out. In... out...

Continue to breathe deeply; noticing how you relax a bit more each time you exhale.

Breathe in... and relax, breathing out.

In... relax...

Breathe... relax...

Keep breathing slowly and calmly. You can relax like this any time you need to. Whenever you want to calm down, you can breathe deeply, and relax... like you are relaxing now. (Pause.)

Now let's begin a guided imagery exercise to allow you to imagine successfully speaking in public, and enjoying the positive experience.

In this visualisation, imagine that everything goes perfectly. Imagine what it would be like to be the most confident, best public speaker in the world.

Create an image in your mind, an image of an excellent public speaker... imagine a confident, well-spoken person... see that this person is you. Picture yourself as a superb public speaker.

Begin to create a mental picture of yourself preparing to give a speech. Imagine that you are preparing in advance to speak. You are feeling confident; excited... you are looking forward to speaking.

After your focused preparation, you are ready to speak. When the day arrives for you to do public speaking, you are excited, eager to begin.

Imagine going to the location where you will speak. See yourself looking forward to speaking. You are excited, eager to talk in public. You can't wait to share your knowledge. You have memorised the words easily, and know that they will come to you exactly as you need them.

Picture entering the location where you will speak, people are gathered to see you. You love it. They can't wait to hear what you are going to say and you can't wait to tell them. Imagine getting up to the front of the room, ready to speak. The crowd waits expectantly.

Picture all the details of this scene. See yourself standing at the front of the room, feeling confident. See the people in front of you, waiting to hear you speak.

Imagine yourself beginning your speech. Confident, your phrases and words are well timed. All throughout your speech, you are breathing calmly, deeply... pausing between each sentence. You maintain a comfortable, smooth rhythm. You talk with smooth, clear speech. Ideas flow. Your hard work and extensive preparation allow your public speaking to be easy, automatic, and almost rote. Everything seems so familiar. It is such a great feeling.

Imagine giving your speech. See yourself as you enjoy this moment. You are confident, comfortable, and having a great time. The anticipatory excitement you felt at the beginning has smoothed into a feeling of confidence and calm.

You feel so at home in front of all these people. They listen, enjoying hearing you speak as much as you are enjoying speaking. You enjoy this experience immensely.

When you reach your conclusion, and speak the final words of your prepared speech, imagine giving the audience time to ask questions. You answer every question easily and proficiently. See your excellent answers satisfying each member of the audience.

The audience is pleased with your performance. You are pleased with your performance. The exhilaration at having completed this public speaking fills you with happiness, contentment, and pride. Notice how fantastic it feels to have shared your unique knowledge to this group of people, knowing we are all unique and special in our own way.

Notice how you can feel confident and calm when doing public speaking. This includes giving prepared speeches, responding to questions; letting the words flow... you are skilled and able to do any sort of public speaking. You are able to relax before, during, and after you speak. You are confident and assertive.

Practicing this visualisation in your mind is like performing actual public speaking. If you are able to do this visualisation and be calm, you can also speak in public calmly. Congratulate yourself for completing this challenge.

Now that you have completed this public speaking guided imagery, take a few moments to reawaken your mind and body... gradually becoming more alert.

Count to 5. When you reach 5, you will be fully awake and feeling calm and energised. Confident in the knowledge you're a special and unique being and have the ability to speak to audiences successfully and confidently.

1   ...becoming more awake and alert
2   ...feeling your mind and body reawaken
3   ...move your muscles a little
4   ...almost completely awake now
5   ...feeling full of energy and refreshed recharged and positive

Guidelines for Creating Healing Imagery
Start with relaxation script:

To begin, choose a comfortable position, seated or lying down. Make sure that you have no distractions around you and are not trying to do anything besides focusing on these words and allowing yourself to become relaxed.

Get comfortable, preparing to relax. Start to relax your body.

Take a deep breath in... and breathe out...

In... and out...

Continue to breathe deeply, slowly, and comfortably.

Count down now, from 10 to 1. As you count each number, you can become more relaxed.

Let's begin.

10 ...let your muscles start to relax...
9 ...the tips of your toes are warming and relaxing spreading gently through your body...
8 ...your muscles are becoming more and more relaxed...
7 ...notice your mind drifting... becoming more relaxed...
6 ...relaxing even further... now... letting... everything go... feeling peaceful...
5 ...a warm feeling of relaxation and love spreading through your body... pleasant and relaxed
4 ...becoming more and more relaxed and peaceful, tranquil...
3 ...free your mind to relax...
2 ...feeling completely relaxed...
1 ...you are now in a deep state of relaxation.

You are very deeply relaxed, comfortable, loved, secure and happy. Allow this feeling of relaxation to grow... becoming even more relaxed... calm and peaceful.

Keep with you the feeling of relaxation, love and security as you think about isolating any illness and understanding every disease has a process which can be reversed. Notice any bad cells as being few in number, small in size, weak in strength, and lacking vividness.

Imagine your immune system as a powerful army which has the intelligence, power and strength to overcome any illness, very intelligent, strong and powerful, large and abundant, understands exactly what to do to reverse any illness, just as it's served you for many years, it can overcome anything.

Believe more in your body's ability to heal than in the disease process, and understand that nothing is fixed – it is a process than can go either way.

Imagine your body's immune system cleansing every cell in your body from the tips of your toes to every part of your body, with the cleansing process you're breathing out any illness in your body in the form of dark smoke floating in the sky, as you do this, the body is realigning itself reversing any disease in your body. Your body's functioning is returning to normal, as you breathe out the rest of your illness.

Your breathing is clear and fresh, and you begin to breathe in clear fresh energy revitalising your body. You now picture yourself healthy, standing strong, you're feeling at peace and relaxed, your body is relaxed and inner organs are running smoothly, any illness is flushed from the body easily and completely.

See yourself accomplishing your goals and fulfilling your life's purpose – thinking about how you would like your future to go. Explore what your ideal future might be and shift your life in that direction so that your immune system responds with you. Draw one or several of your long-term goals that you are moving towards achieving.

Notice how your body and internal organs are functioning smoothly, and your immune system is running in perfect synchronicity with your life's purpose. You are healthy, happy and calm.

Now that you have completed this getting and staying healthy imagery, take a few moments to reawaken your mind and body... gradually becoming more alert.

Count to 5. When you reach 5, you will be fully awake and feeling calm and energised.

1   ...becoming more awake and alert
2   ...feeling your mind and body reawaken
3   ...move your muscles a little
4   ...almost completely awake now
5   ...feeling full of energy and refreshed recharged and positive

Imagery for relaxation

Start by getting comfortable, finding a position, seated or lying down where you can relax. You might want to close your eyes, or focus your gaze on one spot in the room.

Take a deep breath in... filling your lungs... and now breathe out, emptying your lungs completely.

Breathe in again; through your nose... now blow the air out through your mouth.

Breathe in... and out. In... out.

Keep breathing slowly like this, fully emptying your lungs with each breath.

Your deep breathing calms and relaxes you... allows your body to relax.

You can totally relax and let everything go, this is your time, your time to relax and let everything go, relaxing, enjoying this time for yourself. Enjoying being totally relaxed. You deserve this time, and need this time to function at your best. This time of relaxation will allow you to be as calm and healthy as possible. Appreciate yourself for who you are, this relaxation is providing your mind and body the time it needs to balance itself, it is productive, healthy time. You are looking after your health and well-being. Letting everything go, emptying all your thoughts.

As you continue to breathe slowly and comfortably, turn your attention to your body. Notice how you are feeling physically. Simply become aware of the sensations in your body. You can hear and feel your breathing, your heart beating.

You're feeling pleasantly relaxed.

Imagine completely relaxing every part of your body, beginning at the top of your head releasing any tension, breathing out any tension, and relaxing deeper and deeper, and moving downward. Becoming more and more relaxed focusing on your eyes, nose, chin, breathing out tension and feeling more and more relaxed... down to your shoulders. Noticing how your body feels more and more relaxed.

Keep moving down your body, releasing any tension out of every muscle. Feeling more and more relaxed, nearing the centre of your body, at the level of your stomach. Breathing out any tension and becoming relaxed. Continue to relax every part of your body.

Releasing any tension in your hips... breathing out the effects of any tension, becoming further relaxed. Releasing any tension in your knees... becoming more and more relaxed, all the way down to your feet, releasing any tension out of your feet, feeling more and more relaxed.

Take a moment; notice how your body feels to be relaxed. Notice how relaxed you are having released any tension from your muscles, joints, bones, having let all this tension go, feeling totally relaxed.

Focus on how it feels to be relaxed... imagining every muscle in your body releasing every last bit of tension, becoming relaxed... let the tension go, releasing every last bit of tension bit by bit, until you're totally relaxed. Feeling totally relaxed... warming and relaxing.

Notice where your body is the most relaxed. How does the relaxation feel? Imagine that this relaxation is warm and soothing, moving... growing... spreading to relax other parts of your body.

Feel your body becoming more relaxed as the area of relaxation grows to every part of your body.

Imagine that the air you are breathing is pure relaxation. Imagine that the oxygen you breathe in is relaxation, and the carbon dioxide you breathe out is tension. The air exchange is an efficient relaxation system. Feel the relaxation as you take it in through your nose and relax your body, adding to the area of relaxation already there. Expel your body's tension, breathing it out through your mouth. Continue to exchange tension and relaxation. Continue the generalised anxiety relaxation exercise.

Feel the relaxed area getting bigger as you breathe more and more relaxation into your body. Breathe out tension and feel the tension getting smaller.

Breathe in relaxation, and breathe out tension.

Each breath in adds to the relaxation, a full breath more of relaxation is added to your body. Each breath out removes any tension.

Keep breathing in relaxation, and breathing out tension.

You're more and more relaxed with each breath. (Pause.)

Soon the areas of tension are very small. Your breathing can eliminate them entirely. Imagine breathing out any last bits of tension.

You are feeling so calm... so relaxed... breathing in relaxation, and breathing out relaxation. Breathe in... Relax. Breathe out... Relax.

Keep breathing smoothly and regularly, relaxing more and more deeply with each breath.

You are now completely relaxed, calm and at peace.

Feel the warmth as it continues up from your feet, up your legs. Notice the warmth running through your legs.

Feel the core of your body as the warmth coming from your arms and legs meets at your stomach. Feel your core relaxing.

Imagine that your whole body is completely relaxed... enjoying the feelings of relaxation.

Simply rest, enjoying this relaxation. Floating... relaxing.

Focus now on your thoughts. Notice your calm thoughts. Enjoy this relaxation.

Let your mind relax and wander, and as your mind wanders, notice how peaceful you feel.

Now, simply allow your mind to drift. You don't need to focus on anything at all. Just rest, and relax, enjoying this pleasant state you are in.

Keep relaxing for a while longer, enjoying this pleasant, calm feeling. Enjoy the feelings of relaxation.

When you're ready gradually coming back to the here and now, gradually reawakening.

Sit quietly for a moment with your eyes open, reorientating yourself to your surroundings.

Stretch if you want to, allowing your body to reawaken fully. When you are fully awake and alert, you can return to your usual activities, feeling wonderful.

SLEEPING SCRIPT

This guided sleep relaxation script will help you to fall into a deep, restful sleep.

Begin by lying on your back placing your hands in a surrender position. You can change positions any time you need to in order to be more comfortable, but start by lying on your back for now.

Mentally scan your body for areas of tension. Make note of how your body feels. During this sleep relaxation session, you will focus on releasing any tension in your body, and on quietening the mind. Once the mind is calm and peaceful, you will easily drift into pleasant, restful sleep.

Breathe in, drawing in life-giving air and relaxation. Exhale slowly, expelling any tension.

You might have thoughts about things you did today, or things you need to do tomorrow.

Perhaps you are worried about something or someone.

Just imagine emptying all your thoughts into a bag, knowing you can pick the bag up in the morning and revisit your thoughts if you wish.

Now is the time to clear your mind for sleep, so tomorrow you will be refreshed ready for a new day, totally refreshed and positive about the tasks you have throughout the day. Now take a few moments to think about a pleasant experience in your life, reliving the pleasant experience like it's happening in the here and now, notice what you heard, felt, saw, focusing on a pleasant experience. For the next few minutes, let yourself relax and relive a pleasant experience. Really relax and enjoy this time and moment, feeling totally relaxed and at peace, calm.

Notice how your body feels right now.

Where in your body is today's tension stored? Focus your attention on the part of your body that feels most tense. Focus in on one small area of tension. Breathe in deeply, and then let that tension go as you breathe out.

Notice where your body feels most relaxed. Let that feeling of relaxation grow with each breath, spreading further and further the feeling of relaxation.

Feel your attention drifting as you become sleepy and calm.

For the next few moments, you can choose to focus on counting in a relaxing, calm, peaceful voice, and become more relaxed as each number passes through your mind. Concentrate your attention on the number one.

As you count from one to ten, you will become more deeply relaxed. As you relax, you can allow your mind to drift into pleasant, refreshing sleep.

Count slowly with... 1... Focusing on the number 1... 2... you are more deeply relaxed... deeper and deeper... calm. Peaceful. 3... feel the tension leaving your body... relaxation filling your body and mind.

Concentrating just on the numbers, picture in your mind number 4. Very relaxed and calm... the tingly feeling of relaxation in your arms and legs... very heavy... pleasantly heavy and relaxed.

Concentrating on number 5... As you drift deeper... deeper. Calm. Sleep washing over you. Peaceful.

6... deeply relaxed...
7... your body and mind are very calm...
8... so very pleasant and heavy...
9... allowing your mind to drift... easily... no direction... floating... relaxing...
10... you are deeply relaxed...

Now you may count back down from 10 to 1. When you reach 1, you will be fully relaxed and drift into deep sleep. Counting slowly.

Focus only on the numbers and with each number you'll begin to feel more relaxed. Start now at 10... And very slowly focus on...

9... ...as you become deeply relaxed... warm... heavy... peaceful... comfortable... Sleep relaxation...
8; pleasant and calm...
7; drifting...
6; letting go of everything... Sleep relaxation...
5; feeling very good and peaceful... At peace with yourself...
4; feeling sleepy... Deeply relaxed...
3; sleep deeply giving your body time to revitalise... Completely calm and relaxed...
2; feeling completely, relaxed, calm and at peace with the world...
1; feeling warm and calm... Relaxed...

Peaceful... Relaxed...

Allowing you to drift into deep sleep... Deep, pleasant sleep relaxation... Sleep...

Visualising for sport

"Although you can train your body physically by sheer persistence, it's much harder to train your mind... all this visualisation did not come to me in a flash, I had to work at it, and learn how to use it."

Sally Gunnell

Basic picture

Outline the basic content of a match or a technique to be imagined – write it in the first person (I). To describe a skill execution, make sure you include all components of the skill to be imagined or behaviours to be emphasised. Especially if it is a complex skill e.g. taking a free kick, kicking for goal, tennis shot or serve, a golf swing, a snooker shot. If you are describing the events in a sport situation, include all actions that occur in the event and the correct sequencing of all the actions.

➜ Describe the technique in details step by step
➜ Or your role in your team, your game plan

Adding details

Use your senses to fully associate to the experience – any colours around you, sounds, feelings, detail (e.g. context, weather) and movement qualities (e.g. speed of movement). Add the movement or kinaesthetic feelings, physiological or body responses, and the emotional responses. The words that are added are action words such as verbs and adverbs that clearly describe the quality of actions or emotions.

Refine the script

Read it to yourself and imagine the event in all its sensory, action and emotional detail. Do you feel as if you are actually executing the skill or experiencing the event? If not, re-examine the descriptors and action words to see if they accurately reflect the sensations associated with this action.

Tape it

When you have a suitable script then record it on to audio tape and you can then use it as a prompt for your imagery training.

Example – Free Kick in Football

Basic Story – <u>Components</u>: Preparation, football, players around you, goalposts, goalkeeper.

Your technique – to strike the ball look at your target – move into the ball on an angle – keeping your head down, football alongside, the ball pointing in the direction you want it to go, arms out for balance, head down and strike, where you want to place the ball. **Adding detail** – Seeing the ball on the grass and the distance to the goal, striking the ball in the right place, flying into the goal, seeing the position of the goalkeeper, looking at the point on the goal you want to direct the ball.

<u>Script for Striking the Ball in Football</u>

Feeling completely relaxed and confident. Feeling the ground under your feet, seeing the ball clearly on the grass.

Focusing on where you want the ball to go into the goal.

Moving into position to strike the ball.

Moving towards the ball on an angle.

Feeling the power and timing in the body.

Feeling your foot striking against the ball exactly in the spot you want to strike it.

Feeling your body in the correct position following through from the strike.

Watching the ball leave your foot and travel over the wall right in the corner you were aiming for, travelling past the outstretched keeper.

Feeling the ball hit the back of the net and the excitement of scoring a goal.

The same principle as above can be used for any technical aspect of any sport e.g. golf swing, snooker shot, tennis serve.

Imagery can be used in any situation where you want to focus on a specific outcome.

What imagery does; it puts you in the driver's seat, giving you the opportunity to create an outcome you want, giving you the best possible chance to succeed in your task. Imagery is exactly what you make of it. Guided imagery is not mind control. It is a process we do automatically, though rather than leave things to chance, and or let your mind control you, the visualisation process actually gives control back to the individual, making conscious what has been an unconscious process and influence.

Imagery techniques allow for personal changes by changing and growing with you. The more adept you become at image exploration, the stronger your unconscious mind grows, and the more pathways you have at your command.

Chapter 16: Proximity

Your network is your net worth, the people who you associate with will represent who you are emotionally, intellectually, in happiness terms, and financially. If you hang around people who are positive you're more likely to be positive, if you hang around miserable people you're more than likely going to be miserable.

Have you ever been in a good mood and feeling optimistic about things and someone you know phones you up, and you hang up feeling negative; or the other way around, you have had a difficult day and someone's few words of encouragement makes you feel better.

Exercise

Write a list of all the people you associate with during the week.

List the people who have a negative effect.

Write a list of all the people who have a positive effect.

Ensure that you minimise the time you spend with people that have a negative effect on your life. Spend more time with people who have a positive effect on your life, and make the effort to meet as many people as possible which have a positive effect. Misery always looking for new breeding grounds, some people are energy sappers, they drain energy from you. People who always moan are negative, miserable.

Or the type of people you only hear from when they want something, or when things aren't going like they want in their life.

The type of person that breaks up with their partner and is always round telling you how bad men or women are. The type of person who doesn't enjoy their job, and is always round moaning about it and never doing anything about it. Of course you are going to have times where friends and family go through hard times and you want to be there for them, and vice versa. You will always love your family and have a special bond with certain friends, however we all have a choice and life is short.

Life soon passes us by, and finding a balance between the people we associate with will have a major impact on our lives. It amazes me how often people tell their problems to people who can't do anything for them anyway.

They go into the office on Monday and moan about their partner to someone else at work who has relationship problems, and then they go home and moan about work to their partner, who doesn't know anything about their job. Sometimes we have to accept we may not be the best person to give advice on certain subjects. By listening to people run over the same old ground we are not doing them any favours. Sometimes it's worth pointing people into the right direction; professionally for help. After all if someone wasn't feeling well, you wouldn't diagnose them you would advise them to see their GP. To a certain extent the same principle applies to many aspects of life, there are many top professionals out there, like personal trainers for fitness, nutritionists, relationship coaches, careers advisors etc. if someone isn't happy in the place they're in, they need to do something about it. Be wary of being dragged in, as there is only so much support you can give before you become emotionally drained yourself.

The group of people you associate with are going to have a big impact on your life, surrounding yourself with positive energy is the key to happiness.

Chapter 17: Laughter

"Life does not cease to be funny when people die any more than it ceases to be serious when people laugh."
George Bernard Shaw

Have you ever been on a night out, or had a meal with family and friends, gone to watch a show or a film and just laughed so much? One of the best tonics is laughter, and having a good laugh is free. So much money is spent by so many people on products to make themselves feel better. People spend money on cosmetic surgery, intoxicate their bodies with various medications, take illegal substances, we live in a day and age where many people are looking for a quick fix to feel better.

One of the best resources we have is our sense of humour.

Laughter makes you feel good. The good feeling that you get when you laugh remains with you even after the laughter subsides. Humour helps you keep a positive, optimistic outlook through difficult situations, disappointments, and loss. Humour and laughter strengthen your immune system, boost your energy, diminish pain, and protect you from the damaging effects of stress. Best of all, this priceless medicine is fun, free, and easy to use.

If you haven't already watched the film a great film to watch is *Patch Adams* starring Robin Williams, which portrays the life of Patch Adams who would dress up as a clown, entertaining seriously ill patients, with a positive effect.

Adams' ability to make people laugh has lifted the spirits of seriously ill patients around the world.

You might be going through a hard time in your life or you might be thinking it isn't always easy to laugh with today's fast-paced, modern-day society. Here are some tips and exercises you can do which can assist you with a more positive outlook on life and immediately start to make you feel better.

Smile

→ Get into the habit of smiling and sharing a smile with people around you
→ A simple smile can light up a room

Gratitude list:

Write a list of all the things in your life you're grateful to have in your life.

Some of the things we can often take for granted, food, clothes, access to technology, family, friends, being alive.

Spend time with people who enjoy having a laugh.

Have you ever spent time with people who are downbeat and negative? And walked away feeling drained.

Spending time with people who enjoy having a laugh is infectious, and makes you feel better.

Integrate humour into your conversations at work, with your friends, and family.

Some of the best leaders, teachers, coaches, and influential people are people who use humour to get a point across, ease tension, or feelings of any nerves. The effects of a good icebreaker, the positive effects of sharing a joke, seeing the funny side of life is a great way to build rapport and make people feel at ease.

Creating opportunities to laugh

→ Watch a funny film.
→ Go to a comedy show.
→ Read a funny book.
→ Spend time with funny people.
→ Share a good joke or a funny story.
→ Spend time with your children.
→ Do something out of the ordinary.
→ Make time for enjoyable activities (e.g. bowling, badminton, karaoke).

Look at the bright side of life.

Laugh at yourself. Being able to laugh at yourself is an art in itself; sometimes it's easy to take ourselves too seriously.

Attempt to laugh at challenging situations.

Look for the humour in a bad situation; look for something positive to come out of something negative.

Lighten up

Let go of the things that you can't control and focus on your life.

Keep things in perspective

There's no point getting worked up or being too upset about things that don't really matter in the grand scale of things. Sometimes it's worth drawing on past challenges and realising everything is temporary good or bad; with a positive outlook good will come out of every situation. It's not always easy to laugh, however in amongst the face of adversity being able to dust yourself off, put a smile on your face, roll the sleeves up and have a good laugh is often the best way forward.

In the next chapter we will look at letting go of the past and building a brighter future.

Chapter 18: Letting Go of the Past

A young man was getting ready to graduate from college. For many months he had admired a beautiful sports car in a dealer's showroom, and knowing his father could well afford it, he told him that was all he wanted.

As graduation day approached, the young man awaited signs that his father had purchased the car. Finally, on the morning of his graduation his father called him into his private study. His father told him how proud he was to have such a fine son, and told him how much he loved him. He handed his son a beautiful wrapped gift box.

Curious, but somewhat disappointed the young man opened the box and found a lovely, leather-bound book. Angrily, he raised his voice at his father and said, "With all your money you give me a book?" and stormed out of the house, leaving the book.

Many years passed and the young man was very successful in business. He had a beautiful home and wonderful family, but realised his father was very old, and thought perhaps he should go see him. He had not seen him since that graduation day. Before he could make arrangements, he received a call telling him his father had passed away, and had willed all of his possessions to his son.

When he arrived at his father's house, a sudden sadness and regret filled his heart.

He began to clear his father's office and underneath a file saw the still new book his Dad had given to him on his graduation, just as he had left it years ago. With tears in his eyes, he opened the book and began to turn the pages with what was a collage of memories since his birth. As he looked through the pictures, a car key dropped from an envelope taped behind the book. It had a tag with the dealer's name, the same dealer who had the sports car he had desired. On the tag was the date of his graduation, and the words... PAID IN FULL.

How many times in life do we harbour certain thoughts and feelings that are based on our interpretation?

Life is truly an amazing journey, I am sure we have all come across the saying life is what you make it. The one thing for sure in life is no one knows how long we have. If you knew how long you were going to be alive for would it make a difference?

What would you do differently? What could you do differently?

You have got this far reading the book; you have a little further to go, before you embark on your own special journey.

This chapter is about clearing up your past and moving on with a brighter future. Have you ever come across the type of person or people who constantly go on about things in the past and be a major factor in moving on? The story of their past weighs them down like the weight of the earth on their shoulders.

Imagine going back in time to the beginning when we are born, we have a clear mind. Our thoughts, feelings about the world and ourselves are fresh. The game begins; we are on the journey of life. It is from that moment that the person we are takes shape.

The nature versus nurture debate will always rumble on, maybe the person we develop into has a contribution of both.

However one thing's for sure, along the way we develop emotions to certain events and actions that have an impact on our life. You don't have to be a rocket scientist to work out if you were told you were ugly, fat, stupid, crap at sport, a useless idiot, particularly by people you looked up to, it potentially could develop negative emotions about the way you live your life or how you feel about yourself. Or when we watch television, read magazines, we are told live life in a certain way, do certain things, whatever it may be, type of car we should drive, type of house we should live in, furniture we should have, type of hair, clothes, body shape and size, the list goes on, and if you don't conform to what's considered the norm you're left feeling inadequate.

The truth is none of us are perfect, we are human, and we live and learn and make mistakes along the way. Some people continue to live their lives based on just one experience. It only takes one negative comment or one bad experience and it's taken on board as a belief, without even stopping to question the validity or rationality, or the justification of the person saying it.

I once had a client who hadn't been in a relationship for 40 years; in their own words they said they felt worthless. He thought it might have been down to constant verbal abuse he experienced by one of his parents, calling him ugly amongst other things. It is sad the things people say and do to other people, and sometimes when I am working with someone who has grown up under the most difficult of circumstances, suffered physical verbal abuse, or had a negative experience, or experiences, it can make it difficult to move on. People can sabotage their lives on many different levels, personally, professionally, in relationships with feelings of inadequacy.

Though there comes a time that, if we are going to move forward, we need to let go of emotions tying us down from the past.

Technique to clear up negative emotions:

I once did this technique with a woman who had a fear of delivering presentations. She had to deliver an important presentation to a group of around 30 people and she felt quite anxious and nervous about it. She was a very intelligent person, with excellent knowledge on the subject and was confident speaking about what she was going to deliver on a one-to-one basis; however the prospect of delivering a presentation to a group of people made her extremely nervous.

It turns out she was associating negative emotions she had experienced many years earlier when she was in her early primary school years. She had a teacher that would subject the students to humiliation if they got a question wrong by getting them to stand in the front of the classroom and explain their answer.

With that came those same feelings in relation to the prospect of delivering her presentation. So regardless of how much she knew of her content knowledge, was passionate about her subject and enthusiastic, the negative emotions she experienced many years earlier were causing her unnecessary anxiety. So we did the following technique I will demonstrate shortly to clear this negativity up, and she delivered a successful presentation.

You see we are not born with these negative feelings, we develop associations to certain experiences, and some can affect us for a lifetime, if we don't do something about it. Another time on a radio series I was working on, there was a lady who initially came on to the programme to lose weight. Having achieved that goal, she mentioned she had a phobia of swimming, and she tried everything to overcome this. She mentioned a bad experience she had at a swimming pool when she was 8 years old, she was now 64 years of age, and hadn't been to a swimming pool let alone swim for 56 years. She was living her life based on an experience that happened all those years ago. Whatever she tried to do to overcome these feelings did not work. Even though before this negative experience she had some positives, this was the one experience she chose to live her life out of.

She was living her life from the basis of an 8-year-old where swimming was concerned. She wasn't born with this fear, one moment in a swimming pool had stuck in her subconscious and every time she even thought of going for a swim she felt a fear developing.

We did this following technique, and she overcame this fear she had had for over 56 years in less than one hour and booked some swimming lessons, and went swimming thereafter.

I have done this technique with many people over many years helping them overcome negative feelings or attitudes they have which are limiting their life.

Release your negative emotions

Exercise to release negative emotions:

You need a balloon for this following technique.

1. Identify a negative attitude or a feeling you have that is holding you back. An attitude which is preventing you from fulfilling your potential, or achieving a goal, ambition, dream, living the life you deserve. Possibly an attitude which is sabotaging your relationships, stopping you from changing jobs, setting up a business e.g. you're not good enough, you're never going to succeed, you can't find a partner, you're never going to be happy or a story from your past you keep recycling which is not productive.

2a. On a piece of paper or cardboard write down some significant events that have happened in your past, positive and negative, (e.g. first time you fell off a bike, being told off by a parent, getting your driver's license, graduating, your first kiss, breaking up with a partner, a bad holiday, good holiday).

2b. Now write down some of the things you're looking forward in the future, (e.g. travelling the world, writing a book, meeting someone, new job, exciting venture, getting into great shape, meeting exciting people).

2c. Now close your eyes, relax and imagine a line that represents your positive future, placing all the exciting things you're looking forward to on a line that represents time.

2d. Now with your eyes closed imagine the here and now, the present.

2e. With your eyes closed imagine those past events you wrote down, as you imagine all your past events imagine placing them on the line that represents time in your past.

2f. Now imagine joining your line of the future, present and past events.

3. Now remembering that negative attitude or a feeling you have. Imagine going backwards in time identifying times in your past where you had that negative feeling before. At each time you notice those negative feelings, make a mental note and continue backwards to the very first experience you had of that attitude or feeling.

4. When you reach the very first experience of that attitude or feeling, detach yourself from the feeling and look at the memory from the left-hand side.

See your younger self, what happened for you to feel these negative thoughts about yourself and the people around you?

Next step over the timeline to the right and look at the memory from another perspective.

Now imagine floating above the experience as high as you possibly can till you can barely see it.

Now float back down and imagine going to a time shortly before the event which produced those feelings or attitude, you begin to realise those feelings were not always there. There was a time where you didn't have those negative feelings.

Gather all the information about what happened to make you feel this way from different perspectives. Imagine walking or floating back alongside your timeline to the present.

5. As you arrive at the present, look back along your timeline of past events to that very first instance you experienced these negative feeling or attitudes. Determine what resources you have now at the age you are, the life experience and wisdom you now have that would have been useful in that experience when you were younger. When you're young, you do the best you can with the knowledge you have, you are now older and you can deal with those feelings a lot better.

6. Fully associate into the resources you have now e.g. confidence, intelligence, and wisdom. Notice what you see, hear and feel when you're at your best and imagine filling up a bag with all the positive resources you have now, bringing them back to your past.

7. Now bring these resources back to your past. Imagine walking back alongside your timeline in a place immediately before the memory of the past. Imagine passing all these resources back to the person you were when you first had these negative feelings about yourself, passing resources such as confidence, intelligence, experience, wisdom.

8. Having passed those resources to your younger self how is your response different to the experience you had that made you feel inadequate or negative?

   How do you feel differently about yourself?

Now let those negative emotions go, let them go forever. Your mind works to serve you and it may have been holding these thoughts to protect you though now it's time to let go. Now picking up your balloon, exhale all those negative feelings into the balloon. Get rid of those feelings into the balloon, blow it as big as you can, and imagine getting rid of every ounce of those negative feelings or attitude you had. Once you have got rid of the negative feelings, tie the balloon up, and burst those feelings.

Now make your way back to the present having released all those negative feelings, and as you make your way back in time each time you come across the same negative feelings, release them, and replace them with the positive resources. As you make your way back to the present notice how you feel releasing all the negative energy.

9. Having released all the negative energy, imagine how you will respond differently to events and interactions with people. Having released your negative feelings, imagine two weeks into the future, then two months, four months, six months, then one year into the future, laying down these new positive resources at each point.

10.Now from the future face the present and notice the changes you have made with those new positive resources, letting go of the old negative ones. Give your present self whatever information you have that will assist you in making those changes.

Now gradually come back into the here and now into the present feeling positive, refreshed recharged, focused and determined.

Congratulations you have broken free of a negative aspect of your past – now for the future.

Chapter 18: Part Two – The Path We Take

*"Do not follow where the path may lead. Go instead where
there is no path and leave a trail."*

Ralph Waldo Emerson

It takes one moment of inspiration to completely transform
our life.

One phone call, a meeting, a chance encounter, to draw on a
new set of opportunities and create a life of purpose: *If you
keep doing what you have always done in life you will keep
getting the same results, if you want to change certain things
in life you need to do something different.*

Imagine now standing at a fork in the road of your life. You
have come to a decision point. Do you continue to walk
along the same path or do you make new pathways for your
life?

Exercise

**Take five minutes to think about some of the things you
would like to achieve in your life: get into shape, build a
business, new job, study, travel, relationship, some of the
new positive attitudes, resources such as confidence,
motivation, or happiness.**

**Now think about all the things in life you will be missing
out on if you don't change some of your thoughts, feelings
or attitudes.**

Or give some of your goals your best shot.

Take five minutes to write down what you would be missing out on.

Think about how having certain negative beliefs, limiting beliefs, negative behaviours and putting things off has cost you, and caused you pain, in your health, relationships, your life.

Now you stand facing two roads leading to different paths, journeys and destinations.

The road on the left is a slow downward road. It is easy to take the Low Road. You could just coast down it. It is the path of doing what you have been doing for so long. **By continuing doing what you have always done** you will keep getting what you have always got.

The road on the right goes upward. It will take some effort to take the High Road. But, it is the way of freedom, choice and life. It is the road of being in control of your life. It is the High Road to Success! **It is the road you have decided to take by going for your dreams, changing any negative behaviour, being the best you can be.**

Look at the road on the left. It means carrying all of the negative feelings associated with continuing to **put things off, carrying on with living with limiting beliefs and negative behaviours**. Think of how you are losing out in different areas of your life, possibly in your relationships, your health, and your sense of purpose. Really allow yourself to feel the burden of any self-destructive behaviour. Feel your desire to be free from all of the ill effects of hurting yourself **with any negative and limiting beliefs.**

Travel down that low road of living out limitations one more year. Keep travelling down that road and notice after one more year of not making any changes what your life is like.

What have you missed out on because you have continued to **do the same things?**

What opportunities will you have missed out on a year from now?

What will do be doing work wise? Relationships? Your health? Your happiness?

In one year's time how do you expect your life to be, where will you be? What will you be doing?

Imagine looking into a mirror and you see yourself, ask yourself, "Am I pleased with myself with where I am in one year's time by carrying on living the same way?"

Am I happy to have another year of **carrying on doing the same things, having the same thoughts and limitations**? Do I feel better having made this decision to carry on? Do you feel any disappointment continuing to **live this way** for another year?

And in for five more years from now write down where you expect to be in your relationships, health, work and other areas by carrying on taking the same path? How will following the same path affect your life? In five years' time how do you expect your life to be, where will you be? What will you be doing?

Let's look forward to ten years' time how do you expect your life to be, where will you be? What will you be doing by living the same way?

Finally imagine you have reached the end of your existence as it is on earth and on your journey you have lived exactly as you are now.

What have you left behind?

How have you made an impact on the lives of others?

What legacy have you left?

What are your achievements?

What are some of the things you accomplished in life? What are some of the things you wished you did in life? And finally what are people's thoughts about you?

And now we take the other road. The new road.

Exercise

Now imagine taking the initiative and pursuing some of your goals, releasing the negative emotions and limiting beliefs that are stopping you from going forward.

Take five minutes to think about what your life will be like; your health, work, study, travel, relationships.
In a year from now:

➜ **What opportunities have you created for you and other people?**

➜ **What is your sense of purpose?**

➜ **How has your life been different a year from now by taking the new road?**

➜ **What is it like to be in better shape? Have a different job? How are your relationships?**

Now, continuing to stay on the High Road of Success.

Looking forward five years down the line on this road of success.

Take five minutes to think about what your life will be like; your health, work, study, travel, relationships, in five years from now.

➔ **What opportunities have you created for you and other people?**
➔ **What is your sense of purpose?**
➔ **How has your life been different five years from now by taking the new road?**
➔ **What is it like to be in better shape? Have a different job? Your relationships?**

Everything in your life is better for having made these permanent changes. – Enjoy the feeling of knowing that you have made a permanent change, knowing that you will never go back to the old way.

Now let's focus on a 10-year point on this High Road of Success to the 20th year. And there you are after 10 more years of making these good and positive changes in your life. Bring forth all of the effects of these choices. Really allow yourself to feel the effects of these decisions of continuing to follow this new positive path for 10 more years.

Limiting and negative beliefs about yourself are now simply a thing of the past. It was a mistake to have ever **allowed yourself to be bound by these limitations,** now you are free **from the negativity** and will remain free for the rest of your life! You look into that mirror one more time and ask yourself, "Am I pleased with myself for **making these positive choices** for 10 more years? Would I ever go back to that old bad habit of hurting myself by **living with**

limitations? Am I glad that I have made these permanent changes?"

→ **What opportunities have you created for you and other people?**
→ **What is your sense of purpose?**
→ **How has your life been different 10 years from now by taking the new road?**
→ **What is it like to be in better shape? Have a different job? What are your relationships like?**
Finally imagine you have reached the end of your existence as it is on earth and on your journey you have lived your life taking the positive road.

→ What have you left behind?
→ How have you made an impact on the lives of others?
→ What legacy have you left?
→ What are your achievements?
→ What are some of the things you accomplished in life?
→ What are the people who you care about thought's about you?
→ What are your thoughts about how you lived your life?
Congratulations on taking the path of fulfilment and enlightenment.

Life is about choices, we all have a choice, and throughout our lives we will encounter many roundabouts along the way and it is up to us to make a decision. It is amongst these decisions that our destiny is shaped. True success is about living your life like it matters with a sense of purpose and fulfilment.

Now we conclude with a short story and a final word.

87-Year-Old Woman Named Rose

The first day of school our professor introduced himself and challenged us to get to know someone we didn't already know. I stood up to look around when a gentle hand touched my shoulder.

I turned round to find a wrinkled, little old lady beaming up at me with a smile that lit up her entire being.

She said, "Hi handsome. My name is Rose. I'm eighty-seven years old. Can I give you a hug?"

I laughed and enthusiastically responded, "Of course you may!" and she gave me a giant squeeze.

"Why are you in college at such a young, innocent age?" I asked.

She jokingly replied, "I'm here to meet a rich husband, get married, and have a couple of kids..."

"No seriously," I asked. I was curious what may have motivated her to be taking on this challenge at her age.

"I always dreamed of having a college education and now I'm getting one!" she told me.

After class we walked to the student union building and shared a chocolate milkshake.

We became instant friends. Every day for the next three months we would leave class together and talk non-stop. I was always mesmerised listening to this "time machine" as she shared her wisdom and experience with me.

Over the course of the year, Rose became a campus icon and she easily made friends wherever she went.

She loved to dress up and she revelled in the attention bestowed upon her from the other students. She was living it up.

At the end of the semester we invited Rose to speak at our football banquet.

I'll never forget what she taught us. She was introduced and stepped up to the podium. As she began to deliver her prepared speech, she dropped her three by five cards on the floor.

Frustrated and a little embarrassed she leaned into the microphone and said simply, "I'm sorry. I'm so jittery. I gave up beer for Lent and this whisky is killing me! I'll never get my speech back in order so let me just tell you what I know."

As we laughed she cleared her throat and began: "We do not stop playing because we are old; we grow old because we stop playing.

"There are only four secrets to staying young, being happy and achieving success. You have to laugh and find humour every day. You've got to have a dream. When you lose your dreams, you die.

"We have so many people walking around who are dead and don't even know it!

"There is a huge difference between growing older and growing up.

"If you are nineteen years old and lie in bed for one full year and don't do one productive thing, you will turn twenty years old. If I am eighty-seven years old and stay in bed for a year and never do anything I will turn eighty-eight.

"Anybody can grow older. That doesn't take any talent or ability. The idea is to grow up by always finding opportunity in change. Have no regrets.

"The elderly usually don't have regrets for what we did, but rather for things we did not do. The only people who fear death are those with regrets."

She concluded her speech by courageously singing *The Rose*.

She challenged each of us to study the lyrics and live them out in our daily lives.

At the year's end Rose finished the college degree she had begun all those years ago.

One week after graduation Rose died peacefully in her sleep.

Final Word

One of the truly great contributions I intended to **make with this book** is to offer people a means of controlling their own lives. Gone are the days when a person might be stuck in an endless cycle of repetitive behaviours and responses resulting in the tedium of ever-diminishing effectiveness. Seize the moment and live life with a whistle in your tune and a spring in your step, making every moment count. Making the very most of this gift we receive called life.

God bless. May you live a life with peace, happiness and love.

For more information on Jimmy Petruzzi seminars, training and resources:

Website: www.nlp-trainingcourses.com
www.excelwithnlp.com

E-mail: info@excelwithnlp.com

Or if you would like to train with Jim personally, telephone:

0800 955 6808

About the Author

Jimmy Petruzzi has worked in many countries with successful people and businesses, including Premiership football teams, top athletes, politicians, entrepreneurs and stars of the small screen, helping them to achieve peak performance in all aspects of their lives.

Jim trains many of the top champions in the world of sport based in the UK, and abroad, and has implemented many of his unique and breakthrough concepts in athletic performance.

Jim works with elite sports performers including, among others, Premiership footballers and teams, he has assisted to prepare international teams for major tournaments such as the soccer World Cup also trained rugby players, European Tour golfers, World and Olympic medallists, international athletes, cricket players, tennis players, professional football and sporting teams and establishments.

Jim has taken these principles of success in sport with NLP and transferred them to the corporate sector with great success. Presently regarded as one of the most successful and effective business coaches and trainers, helping companies increase sales, improve leadership and management skills, set inspiring goals and fulfil their potential, become highly motivated and function effectively as a team.

Jim appears regularly on television and radio in the UK, Australia and the USA, including weekly segments on radio skysportsradio.com Australia radio, Realcoachingradio.com.

He features in worldwide newspapers as well as sports-related documentaries. He is also often asked to provide commentary for radio and in the press, a regular columnist on magazines such as *Peak Performance*, *Men's Fitness* and *Fit Pro*.

He was a writer for INPLTA and the British Association of NLP, a frequent contributor to other publications, as well as a sought-after industry speaker who regularly presents at the leading conferences in the field.

Director of the International Association of NLP and Coaching he received the highly commended for coaching award 2006, for his international and domestic work.

Under Mark Hughes' management at Blackburn Rovers in November 2006, Jimmy Petruzzi delivered NLP training to Blackburn Rovers FC helping them turn their season around.

Testimonials

"Jimmy was a pivotal part of all the football programmes broadcast on Sky Sports Radio between 2006-2011. His insightful understanding and detailed analysis were integral to the success of the Football at Five show which was broadcast five times a week as well as the Live and Exclusive coverage of the 2009/10 English Premier League. Jim also played a key role in the daily World Cup show in 2010. I look forward to future collaboration with Jim in any football show I present or produce."

Andrew Paschalidis

Football presenter, Sky Sports Radio & Racing

"My Son has visited Jim every pre-season for the past 4 years and it has changed his life. With Jim's help, advice and training my son has been able to achieve his goals in becoming a professional footballer. We still visit Jim every year, for a TOP-UP SESSION. Me and my son would recommend Jim to everyone he is an amazing person."

Paul Lynne

"Jimmy is a dedicated professional who integrates NLP, and psychological strategies with physical conditioning to excellent effect. Jimmy is extremely knowledgeable and a leader in his field."

Tony Strudwick,

Head of Fitness and Conditioning, Manchester United FC

"I attended a course hosted and run by Jimmy on NLP. During the course I discovered powerful techniques on how to not only set goals, Jimmy provided a quick and easy to implement set of tools which ensured that I took action to achieve whatever goals I set myself. Since attending the course 2 years ago I have achieved each and every goal which I have set myself. Thanks Jimmy, I hope to attend another one of your courses in the near future."

James Briers

Director, Nanomesh Ltd

"I started training with Jimmy & Sara at 62 years of age, working them has truly transformed my life. I lost 3 stone got into my best shape ever, & overcame a phobia of swimming I had since I was 8 years old."

Margaret S

(BBC GMR)

"Petruzzi an Australian, is one of the best qualified coaches of his kind in the world. He has worked with several top teams including West Ham and Crystal Palace and his advanced training methods look like paying dividends on the pitch... The lads have taken to him and shown belief in his methods but his work is structured and a long-term thing."

Chris Casper

(Former Manchester United Player, Bury F.C. Manager)

Quote from Bury Times

"In recent seasons, the likes of Dave Nugent, Colin Kazim-Richards, Simon Whaley and Tom Kennedy have all come through the youth system to make an impact in the first team and go to play for Championship clubs and England

U21, the strength of the Bury youth system is something Jim must take credit for."

Ross Johnson

Former Bury F.C Director

"Jim's style of teaching surpasses excellence. A massive thank you for helping me on my own personal journey, for my learning and my continued learning. The programmes you taught are excellent, very intellectually stimulating, and I have found as a result of completing the course, that I use what we learnt daily in both home and work life. It has definitely shaped me and become a big part of who I am today. Thank you."

David Go'shay